INVESTIGATIONS

Dedicated to Haim Belzberg. Immigrant, engineer, father.
His contributions to family and country are immeasurable.

INVESTIGATIONS

SELECTED WORKS BY
Belzberg Architects

with essays by
Cindy Allen, Sarah Amelar,
Sam Lubell, and Hagy Belzberg

New York · Paris · London · Milan

1
2
3
4
5
6
7
8
9
10
11
12
13
14
15

Introduction
BY HAGY BELZBERG
7

Brave, Bold, and Beyond
BY CINDY ALLEN
9

The Illusion of Simplicity
BY SAM LUBELL
10

INVESTIGATIONS

1 Ahmanson Founders Room
16

2 Skyline Residence
30

3 Conga Room at L.A. Live
46

4 Holocaust Museum LA (formerly Los Angeles Museum of the Holocaust)
60

Fluid Dynamics
BY SARAH AMELAR
80

5 Kona Residence
86

6 McKinnon Center for Global Affairs
98

7 Gores Group Headquarters
110

8 The Pavilion at City of Hope
128

9 Tree Top Residence
142

10 Threads
156

11 Profiles
172

12 Camelback Residence
190

13 USC Shoah Foundation— The Institute for Visual History and Education Global Headquarters
206

14 BAR Center at the Beach
224

15 Apertures
240

Project Chronology
264

Staff: Past and Present
268

Acknowledgments
270

Author Biographies
271

Belzberg Architects' 20th Street Offices in Santa Monica interweave zoning, community, and green building considerations to create an efficient, multiuse project on a compact lot.

INTRODUCTION
Hagy Belzberg

There has long been an inherent tension in architecture between artistic expression and constraint. Navigating between these often opposing forces is where I live. On the one hand is the inherent need for creative expression—often finding inspiration in the exquisite beauty of the sequential patterns found in nature. On the other are the immediate constraints of program, and more broadly those of economics, both environmental and social. It is often believed that the tension between these elements can be oppressive and antithetical to the creative process. I disagree. As an architect and founder of a design studio, I believe that it is exactly this often messy interplay that forces high-quality, creative, and innovative design. It is only by distilling these competing influences through a collaborative process, with a truly extraordinary group of architects and designers, that we have arrived at the alchemy that is now Belzberg Architects.

Our practice is an ongoing experiment. As a community of designers, we share a desire for discovery, which frequently requires us to challenge established principles, and this drive is also emboldened by our fiercely democratic process. This methodology keeps our work fluid and fresh. It has also enabled us to maintain and grow our core group of associates, all of whom have agency to develop their own interests and pace. Shared aims paired with unconventional practices ultimately allow us to achieve moments of genuine creative elation. Such moments are fleeting and cannot easily be recreated. Yet with each new project lies the potential to unearth another discovery. By testing, trial-and-error, imagination, and a genuine sense of play, the designers, architects, and tinkerers at Belzberg Architects seek to interrupt, disrupt, transition, or layer given patterns to create a complexity that is intended to support moments of exceptional experience.

By viewing projects as springboards for investigations, our office voraciously pursues any opportunity for discovery. This is true whether we are designing an immersive spatial experience through a home, museum, or workspace, or an actual construction methodology.

Another hallmark of our firm is our almost fanatical investigation into making and exposing the unique within the standardized during the various stages of our creative process. It is through this journey, one of exploring the very limits of materials, design, and often engineering, that we find our passion. We accept the years-long immersive exercise within each project, which involves the challenges of developing a substitute means of construction and innovative methodologies with materials, and ultimately culminates with the procession of spaces within the built condition.

Throughout the evolution of our projects, the design process has further led us to experimentation with digital fabrication and unitized material applications. It is never a linear course: our guiding principle is to study the results developed, and subsequently, to adapt what we have learned through our own means of exploration—and then, on to the next examinations.

The ensuing pages are a chronological assessment of selected projects chosen to illuminate the course Belzberg Architects has followed over the past twenty years. With collective curiosity as our beacon, and the freedom to create boldly without any predetermined narrative, we are, gratefully, ever evolving.

BRAVE, BOLD, AND BEYOND
Cindy Allen

When I became editor-in-chief of *Interior Design*, way back at the turn of the millennium, I flew out from New York to Los Angeles to get the lay of the land, and that's when I discovered—and was intrigued by—Belzberg Architects, a fledgling firm at the time. Then, a while later, our L.A.-based deputy editor, Edie Cohen, sent me pictures of the Lab at Belmar, a nonprofit gallery in a mixed-use development near Denver. The design announced the storefront's presence with a fiberglass form that started as an entry canopy, then swooped inside, its glossy whiteness offset by accents in juicy chartreuse. Perfect, I thought, for our Art Issue in 2007. It took only two more years for the firm to grace our cover.

Since then, I have been proud to publish a series of Belzberg projects that can safely be described as spectacular sculptures in their own right. Among them, a gazebo in the form of a parabola welcomes us to a Hawaiian vacation home; an interactive media wall undulates through the lobby of an academic building at Los Angeles's Occidental College; in Mexico City, dynamic facades are the defining feature of a group of office buildings—from swirling aluminum strips the Belzberg team calls "threads" to a honeycomb of masonry block.

The firm is not all about the wow, though. There's a very thoughtful, meditative side that makes itself evident at the award-winning Holocaust Museum LA (formerly Los Angeles Museum of the Holocaust). It's sited underground, in a park, so that visitors descend into darkness before finally reemerging into daylight and nature, a journey of remembrance and healing. When Hagy and I walked through the museum together, we happened to meet a Holocaust survivor also visiting, and the entire experience moved me to tears—that's the power of design.

In 2014, when I visited the firm's studio, I had a camera crew in tow to shoot a documentary on Hagy that would be shown at the ceremony inducting him into *Interior Design's* Hall of Fame. The place is a combination studio-laboratory-clubhouse with surfboards propped against the wall and complex ideas practically flying off the flashing monitors, always two steps ahead of the expected. At the ceremony, when called up to the podium to take a bow in front of a packed audience in the Waldorf-Astoria grand ballroom, Hagy didn't hesitate to share the spotlight, stopping the applause to snap the photo he'd promised his two children and acknowledging the "tinkering geniuses" that collaborate with him at Belzberg Architects.

I continue to champion the firm's work within the design community and beyond, and we are surely kindred spirits, unable to resist the urge to try something new. You never know what you're going to get from Belzberg Architects, but you can always expect to be surprised, then delighted, and finally elated seeing Hagy and his team move great design into the future.

Belzberg Architects' workspace features floor-to-ceiling ocean views. Walls and ceilings are lined with mock-ups from the office's long history of creating innovative material assemblies.

THE ILLUSION OF SIMPLICITY
Sam Lubell

The duality of simplicity and complexity dominates our world. Effective natural systems, social frameworks, and the human body itself are all elegantly simple and impossibly intricate. The world's greatest art can be easy to comprehend, yet often entails limitless complex machinations. The most revolutionary ideas, from the telephone to the iPhone, appear straightforward; but they are generally built from years of accumulated expertise.

This is the essence of Belzberg Architects. The firm's remarkable talent lies in exploring complex, unconventional methods—iteratively merging digital and analog, creating customized kits of parts, researching innovative materials (or adapting familiar materials in new ways), tackling challenging sites, exploring new labor chains, creating flexible, nimble solutions—that explore the edges of design and construction. By boldly and thoroughly facing complexity, they paradoxically mitigate it, making the results seem seamless, simple.

Working with a collaborative, multidisciplinary approach, layered with construction expertise, narrative, and passionate energy, the firm's work is reductive in the same way that the body is reductive: wasting nothing; beautifully built to serve the precise needs of its incorporator. The results are hard-won, not capricious or haphazard. They represent the inevitable, uplifting resolution of complex challenges.

Firm founder Hagy Belzberg grew up steeped simultaneously in function and poetry, simplicity and complexity. His father, Haim, was an engineer, designing nuclear reactors at California Institute of Technology (Caltech) and NASA's Jet Propulsion Laboratory; making the impossible possible. His mother, Malka, a sculptor, crafted elegant works in bronze starting in his childhood. From the beginning, Hagy saw things differently. He loved architecture—its forms, masses, and poetry. But he grew just as fascinated with its complex systems and often unrecognized forces: its engineering, technology, building systems, and subtle articulations; the negative spaces it carved out, the feelings it provoked.

The Mataja Residence (RIGHT) and Flint Peak Residence (BELOW) are both early examples of challenging sites and share a contrasting mix of light roof structures, large glass walls, and heavy foundations.

Belzberg launched his firm by exploring opportunities on intensely challenging sites—mountain bluffs and steep foothills that were considered unbuildable. In response, he installed thick concrete retaining walls to keep water and earth from encroaching; long steel and concrete cantilevers, extending from building masses to create sweeping views; honeycombed, double concrete slabs to bolster structure, protect and organize utilities, and blend with surroundings. The results were soaring projects like the Mataja Residence in Malibu and the Flint Peak Residence in Pasadena that seem to take off from their steep perches. Large glass walls and projecting masses create a simple lightness and ethereality that belie the complex, heavyweight solutions required to make them possible.

Such work, harnessing intense complexity to achieve powerful simplicity would set the tone for the firm's future endeavors. The results—exuberant, free-spirited architecture that was in reality highly prescribed—paved the way for subsequent expansion into commercial, institutional, and hospitality sectors, in all types of environments, each with its unique set of challenges and solutions.

The firm's development of efficient kits of parts—fusing high- and low-tech, complex form with simple repetition, straightforward structure with complex configuration—is one of its mainstays for mitigating complexity. It starts with intense research and iteration and ends with a way forward that is legible, simple, and often more affordable.

This approach permeates the Conga Room at L.A. Live, a popular Latin music and dance venue in downtown Los Angeles packed with dance floors, VIP areas, a restaurant, and several bars. To inject a lively, sensuous vitality, provide acoustic control, and blend varied spaces, the firm topped the venue with a surface of dozens of triangular computer numerical control (CNC)-milled painted plywood panels. These pieces—lightweight, and inexpensive—appear to be united into a flowing, rhythmic whole. But they're actually quite different: each shifts in angle and porosity, reflecting or absorbing the club's rhythmic sounds and vibrant lighting. Their organization was executed via parametric software, highly responsive technology pinpointing placement according to specific functional requirements.

ABOVE: The Gores Group Headquarters (ABOVE LEFT AND CENTER) and the Holocaust Museum LA (ABOVE RIGHT) feature the innovative synthesis of traditional construction techniques and digital fabrication.

Similar thinking transformed the Gores Group Headquarters in Beverly Hills, a renovated 1960s commercial office building whose undulating glass and concrete surface consists of a kit of just three slumped panels, fabricated off-site, flipped and rotated to make each seem unique, and installed like a standard storefront system. The panels also perform as a second facade, providing thermal and acoustic insulation for a building located on a busy stretch of the city. Inside, the firm carved out a curved, sensuous atrium and interior stair, whose steam-bent ash-wood slats were computer-modeled and fabricated off-site, then assembled like puzzle pieces. The project is topped with a "fifth facade," a large roof-deck shaded by an undulating, prefabricated metal canopy, once again created off-site and pieced together on-site. It is yet another example of customization, then systemization; prefabrication, then large-scale production, employed as powerful tools.

Another tool that the firm employs to solve intricate challenges is working outside the boundaries of traditional construction—its familiar contractors and suppliers, its predictable techniques and expectations. For the Holocaust Museum LA (formerly Los Angeles Museum of the Holocaust), embedded in the city's Pan Pacific Park, Belzberg Architects worked to create a historical narrative: descending below the earth, hearing the sounds from the nearby park, but being unable to share in them. To create this undulating, underground condition, the firm collaborated with a shotcrete contractor that often builds swimming pools. Belzberg Architects CNC-printed uniquely shaped stencils that were transferred to plywood templates and used by its collaborators to shoot the building's concrete form, which was hand-trawled to a smooth surface. It was an adapted process—employing a familiar technique (for the contractor) and employing it in a new way. The unique collaboration solved issues of both complexity and budget. It meant designing to the team's specialties, finding opportunity where it is usually unexplored.

ABOVE: The Ahmanson Founders Room benefits from the early adoption of CNC tools used with off-the-shelf building materials, and takes advantage of the natural warm tones of the Douglas fir glulam beams.

The firm continues to challenge the outdated siloes of construction, refining techniques, layering knowledge and lessons. Mexico City, long a bastion of architectural experiment—from Félix Candela and Luis Barragán to, more recently, Tatiana Bilbao and Enrique Norten—has become one of Belzberg Architects' chief test labs. Common expertise, materials, and techniques are exploited and employed in new ways. Threads, an office building adjacent to Paseo de la Reforma, pushes its utility core to the structure's edge, opening the floor plates to flexible configuration, including exterior communal areas, which are accentuated by vertical aluminum elements that appear contiguous across the various floors. In actuality, these "fins" were digitally designed to connect to the slab, glazing, and balconies. They appear to intersect, prefabricated and assembled on-site to create the illusion of singularity. A hospitality project, Apertures, relies on a screen of clipped-together, canted or angular concrete blocks—a regularly used construction method at Belzberg Architects—tweaked to form a sculpted buffer, curving on multiple planes and shaping and directing views. As usual, the firm was inspired by common materials and techniques to create something both unconventional and utterly practical.

The firm has always searched for new materials, new approaches, new ideas, continually finding ways to reduce complexity that result in purer solutions. But this functionality has never been boring. It has always been infused with drama: rhythm, narrative, and exuberance. The Ahmanson Founders Room, buried beneath Los Angeles's Music Center, channeled this type of energy. Rippled, CNC-milled Douglas-fir, walnut, and fiberboard surfaces—fabricated off-site and acting as acoustic isolators—serve as room dividers and ceilings, billowing like theater curtains and sound waves; torqueing like dancers on the stage above. The practical became ethereal, lending energy and movement. Perforated wood wall panels, also prefabricated, add another layer of drama; backlit, they allow light to filter in like a constellation of stars.

This flair for the dramatic, flowing from people, place, and system, is embedded in every Belzberg project. A site's angled topography is reflected in a home's sculptural surfaces. Perforated carbon steel and shimmering electrostatic paint accentuate a torquing facade. Geometric graphics convey structural intensity. Luminous bands of light make interlocked and cantilevered surfaces appear to float. The Conga Room's expertly arranged pieces are more than functional: they interact with the audience below them. The Holocaust Museum LA is a structural innovator, but it gains power and narrative in its haunting forms, merging with the earth.

To dream up and realize this collection of experiments, the firm relies on an approach in which all voices are heard, but ideas don't get lost in the din—another form of managing complexity. With each subsequent experiment, project teams become more confident, able to take more risks. Slight tweaks to existing typologies and construction methods can add up to major changes in form and program, and those adjustments become more pronounced with each success.

Evolving in this way has led to bolder iterations, across all types of program, many evidenced in this book. Yet while complex and daring, the resulting projects are refined in a way that almost hides the churning that enables them. This can, ironically, present a challenge when it comes to publicity. How can the public fathom the intense machinations that go into making something seem so simple? A picture never tells the full story.

But the true reward, and inspiration, is the resolution: the elegant mastery of a seemingly insurmountable challenge. "So many things are possible as long as you don't know they are impossible," author Mildred Taylor once said. Belzberg Architects will continue to evolve, testing the boundaries of experience, imagination, and, yes, possibility. But this journey will always be rooted and driven by practicality. Nothing profound comes out of thin air.

OPPOSITE: The slumped-glass facade at the Gores Group Headquarters was created by reappropriating an auto manufacturing technique.

PREVIOUS PAGES: The gradient depth of carved wood, which tapers from flat at the rear of the Ahmanson Founders Room and on the side edges, to deep grooves at the front of the room and in the center, flows continuously from ceiling to wall.

ABOVE: The founders enter the space directly from the parking garage; the private entrance comprises backlit, perforated wood panels.

Ahmanson Founders Room

LOS ANGELES, CALIFORNIA, U.S.A.
2004–2006

The Ahmanson Founders Room honors the original and current donors of The Music Center, downtown Los Angeles's multidisciplinary performing arts center. This 2,500-square-foot retrofit project inserted an exclusive antechamber within the framework of the existing Ahmanson Theatre basement, adding a new lounge and bar for members. Located off the first level of subterranean parking, the design creates a stark contrast to its context, signally a discrete experience prior to a performance.

The entrance, marked by a floor-to-ceiling perforated screen, introduces the sculpted texture of wood that prevails throughout the space. Inside, visitors are greeted by a series of off-the-shelf, repurposed, glued, laminated (glulam) Douglas fir beams that have been carved using a computer numerical control (CNC) router. The ripple pattern, which begins in the ceiling of the main room, folds and appears to cascade to the floor, framing the entrance. The panels above are hung like tiles and sanded by hand to mask the seams, allowing the undulation to come to the fore. Walls also feature CNC-perforated medium-density fiberboard (MDF) panels that were CNC-carved with a grid of three-dimensional pyramids to create a tufted texture. The perforated pattern of these pieces echoes the ceiling while cove up-lighting behind them help expand the appearance of the room's overall height and width. Similar fabrication techniques have been applied to custom, modular furniture pieces throughout. The unique treatment of standard, off-the-shelf materials transforms what was previously storage space to stunning visual effect and elevates the transitional space between parking and theater.

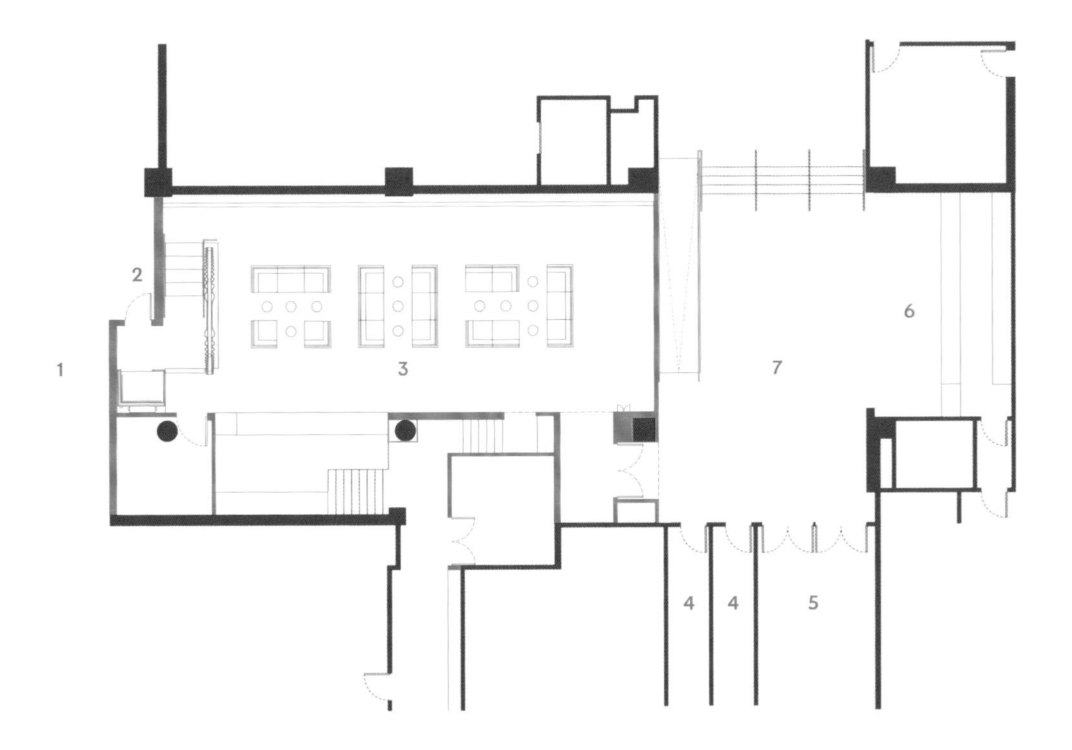

FLOOR PLAN
NEW
EXISTING
1 GARAGE
2 GARAGE ENTRANCE
3 FOUNDERS ROOM
4 BATHROOM
5 THEATER ENTRANCE
6 ENTRY VESTIBULE
7 LOBBY

0 16FT

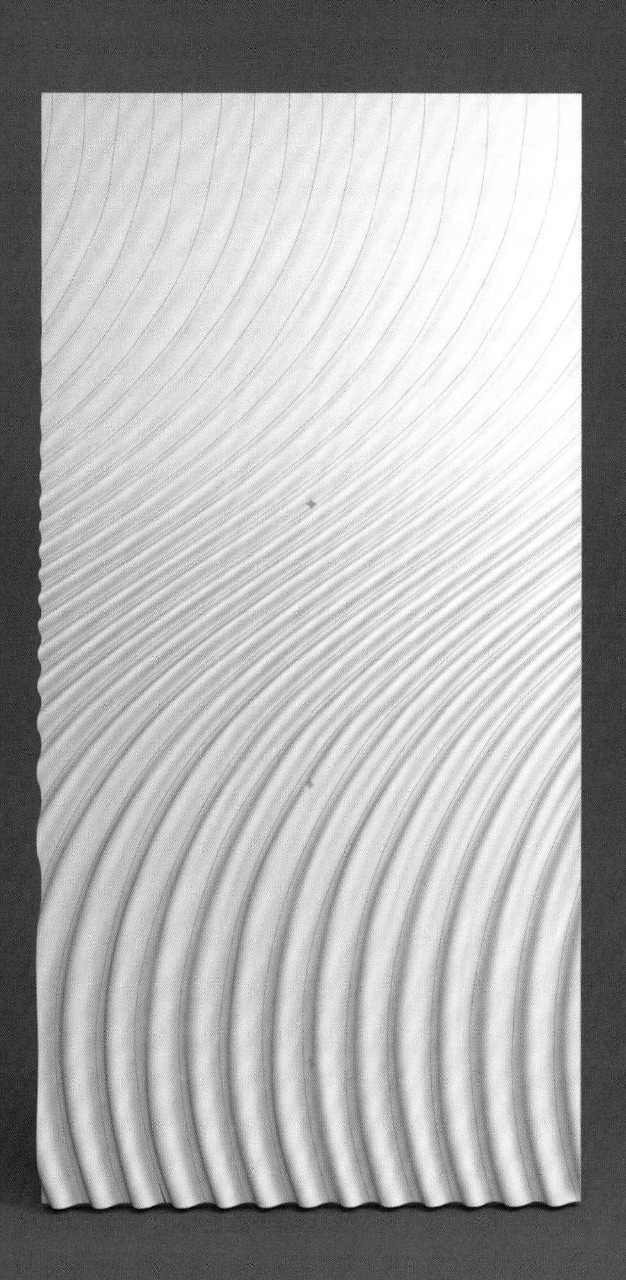

OPPOSITE: Carved three-dimensional depth and perforated moiré are opposing techniques applied to animate surfaces.

ABOVE AND LEFT: Each ceiling panel is unique and CNC-carved from off-the-shelf Douglas fir glulam beams, then hand-finished to align with adjacent panels to create the unified undulating surface.

Each 24- by 48-inch wall panel is also unique. The perforation pattern mimics elements of the ceiling design and was drilled with seven holes of different diameters, while another layer of routing creates a tufted texture.

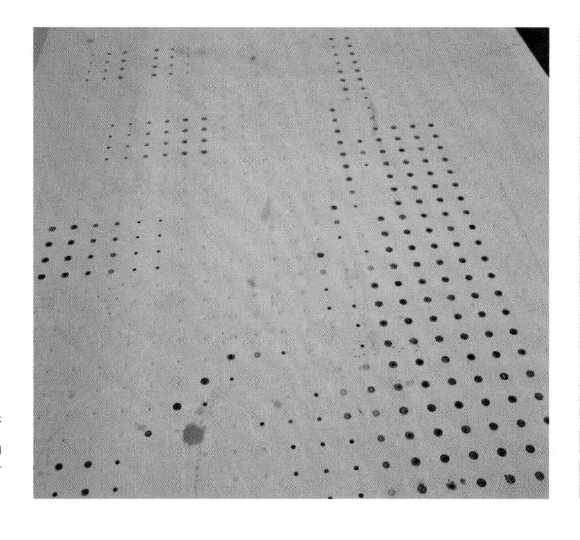

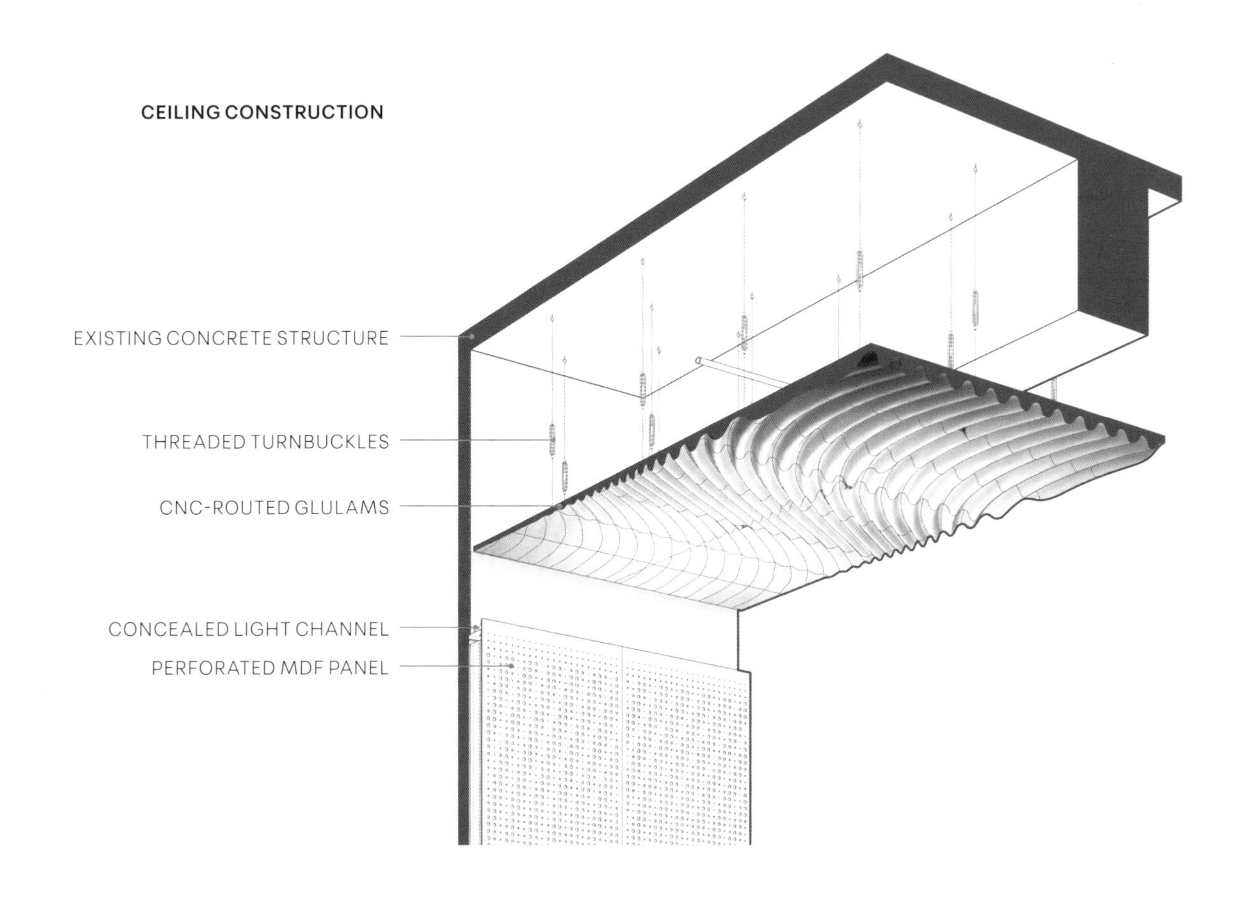

The diagram of the ceiling assembly mock-up (ABOVE) and the in-progress installation (LEFT) show the simple hanging system.

OPPOSITE: Rounded corners at the intersection of four ceiling tiles reveal pin lights, sprinklers, and other systems, with minimal disruption.

OPPOSITE: The vertical entry partition that divides the lounge space and the entry vestibule is created from a double-sided series of carved panels.

BELOW: Custom walnut sectional sofas with smooth leather seating surfaces can be rearranged in any number of combinations.

ABOVE: The entry is illuminated with backlit perforated panels, giving depth to the walls.

OPPOSITE: The dramatic entry to the garage is divided by an undulation in the ceiling.

The machine-tufted, backlit, perforated wall panels conceal a hidden light cove at the top, illuminating the edge of the ceiling and amplifying its edge-to-center gradient texture.

2

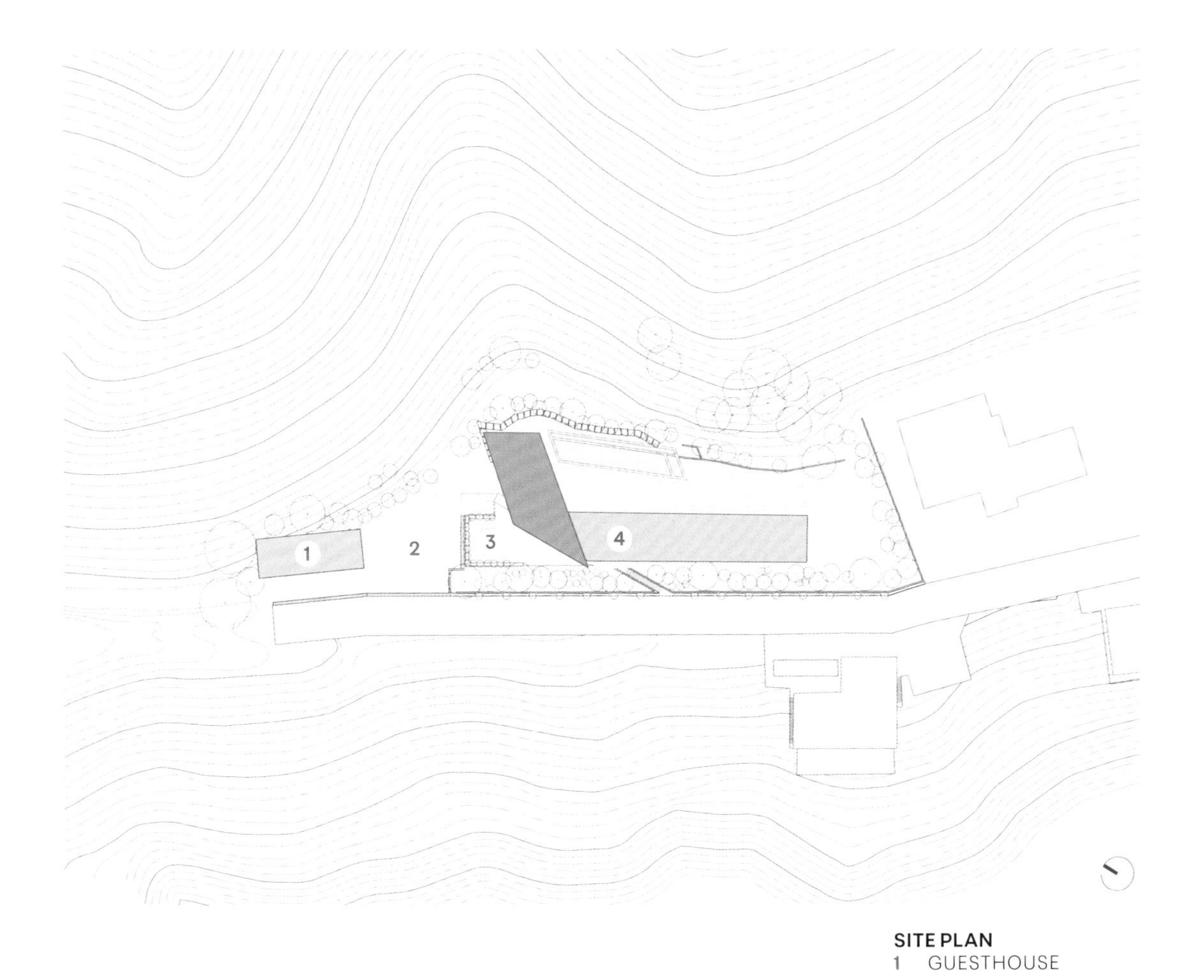

SITE PLAN
1 GUESTHOUSE
2 AUTO COURT
3 VIEWING DECK
4 MAIN HOUSE

Skyline Residence

LOS ANGELES, CALIFORNIA, U.S.A.
2002–2007

The location of the Skyline Residence presents both an impressive opportunity and a sizable challenge. The previously undeveloped site is perched atop the Hollywood Hills with unobstructed views of downtown Los Angeles, Laurel Canyon, and the San Fernando Valley. However, the project was restricted by the long and narrow ridgeline, which was flanked on all sides by steep, brush-covered slopes, and dense granite just below the surface limited the possibility of excavation. Despite (or perhaps because of) these constraints, the project's simple geometry has been able to achieve its striking form.

The 5,800-square-foot residence comprises two buildings that form an efficient, linear footprint intersected by an auto court. The adjacent volumes share a formal language, folding onto themselves to create a contiguous surface—from foundation to protective exterior wall to roof. To protect from direct sun exposure, both structures feature matching lapped screens of Extira slats (a low formaldehyde-emitting composite lumber) to the southwest, and in the main house, the circulation corridor runs along the same side of the building to provide a buffer. Both buildings also use low-emissivity glass throughout, greatly reducing heat gain without compromising the spectacular views to the city below.

PREVIOUS PAGES AND OPPOSITE: The Skyline Residence is sited at the crest of the ridge, and at night appears as a beacon on the surrounding hillside.

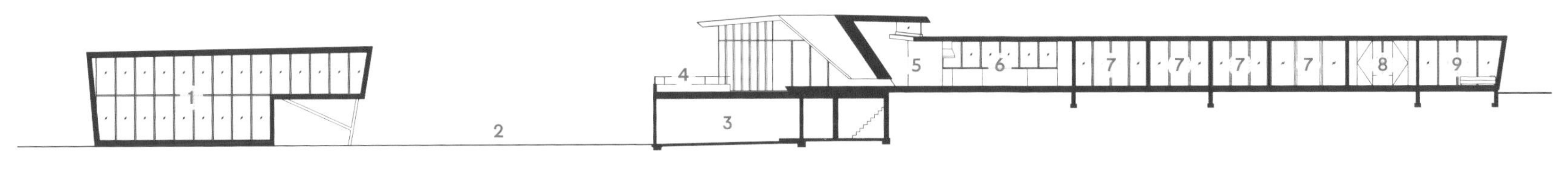

SECTION
1 GUESTHOUSE
2 AUTO COURT
3 GARAGE
4 OUTDOOR VIEWING DECK
5 HALLWAY
6 KITCHEN
7 BEDROOM
8 MAIN BATHROOM
9 MAIN BEDROOM

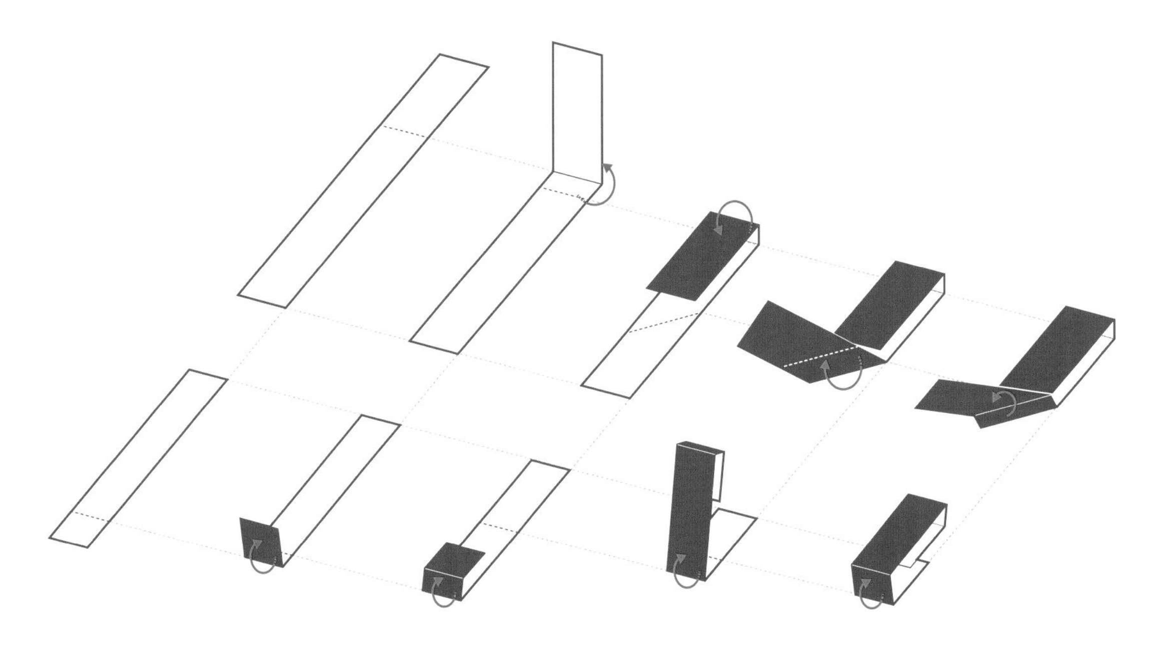

The form of the Skyline Residence is derived from folded planes that provide privacy and protect the building from direct sunlight. The steel framing supports these origami-like folds.

Panoramic views span the San Fernando Valley to downtown.

The intersection of the folded planes creates unique geometries.

The wall that folds to the roofline appears to float at the entry and also highlights the dynamic form of the house.

ABOVE: The outdoor lounge serves as a viewing deck for films projected on the outside of the adjacent guesthouse (OPPOSITE).

An ode to Case Study House #22 (the Stahl House), the Skyline Residence creates an iconic moment overlooking the city.

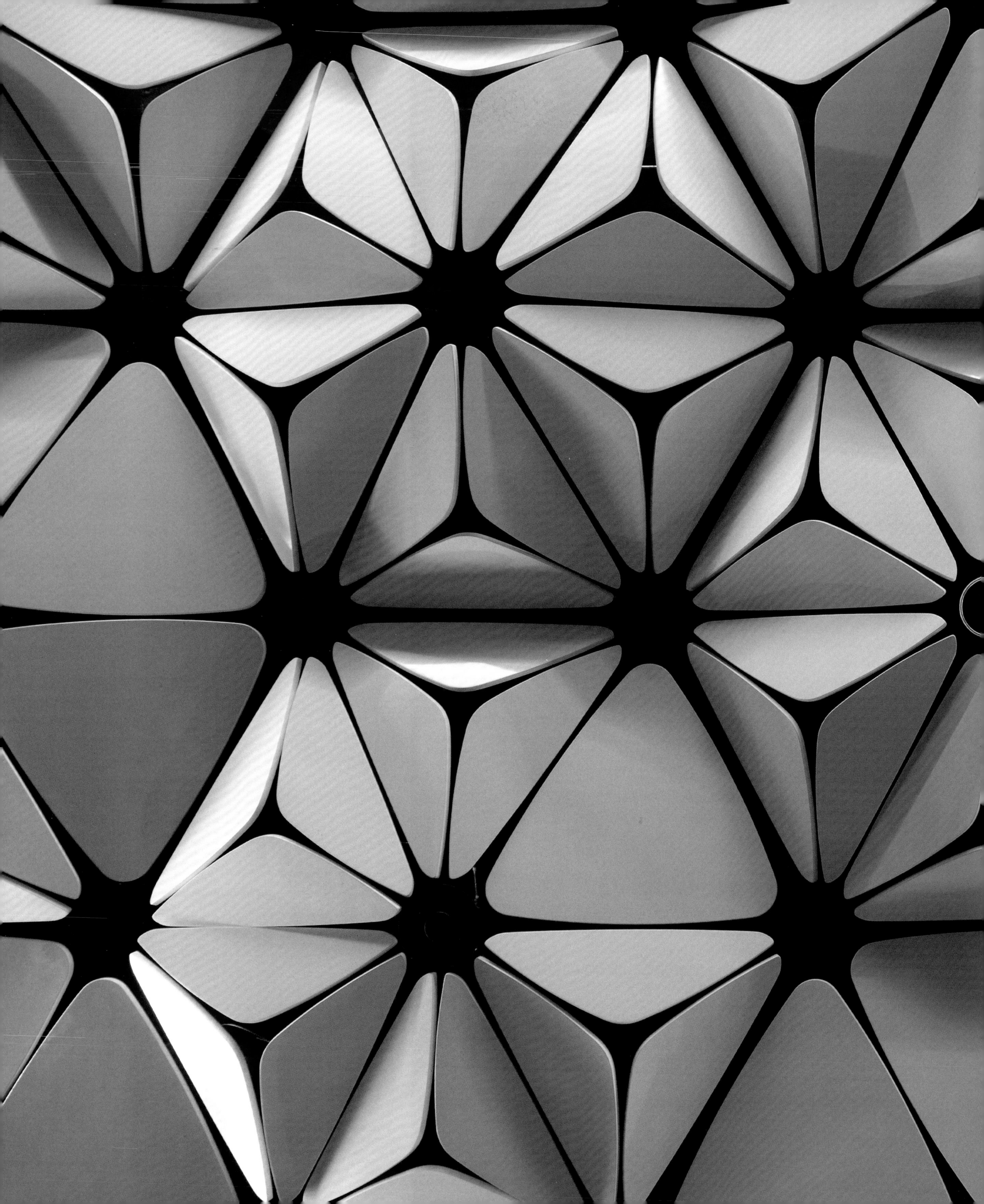

3

The dynamic ceiling system of the Conga Room at L.A. Live (PREVIOUS PAGES) intensifies at certain moments in concert with bold manipulations of the solid architecture, such as a large void carved into the floor (ABOVE).

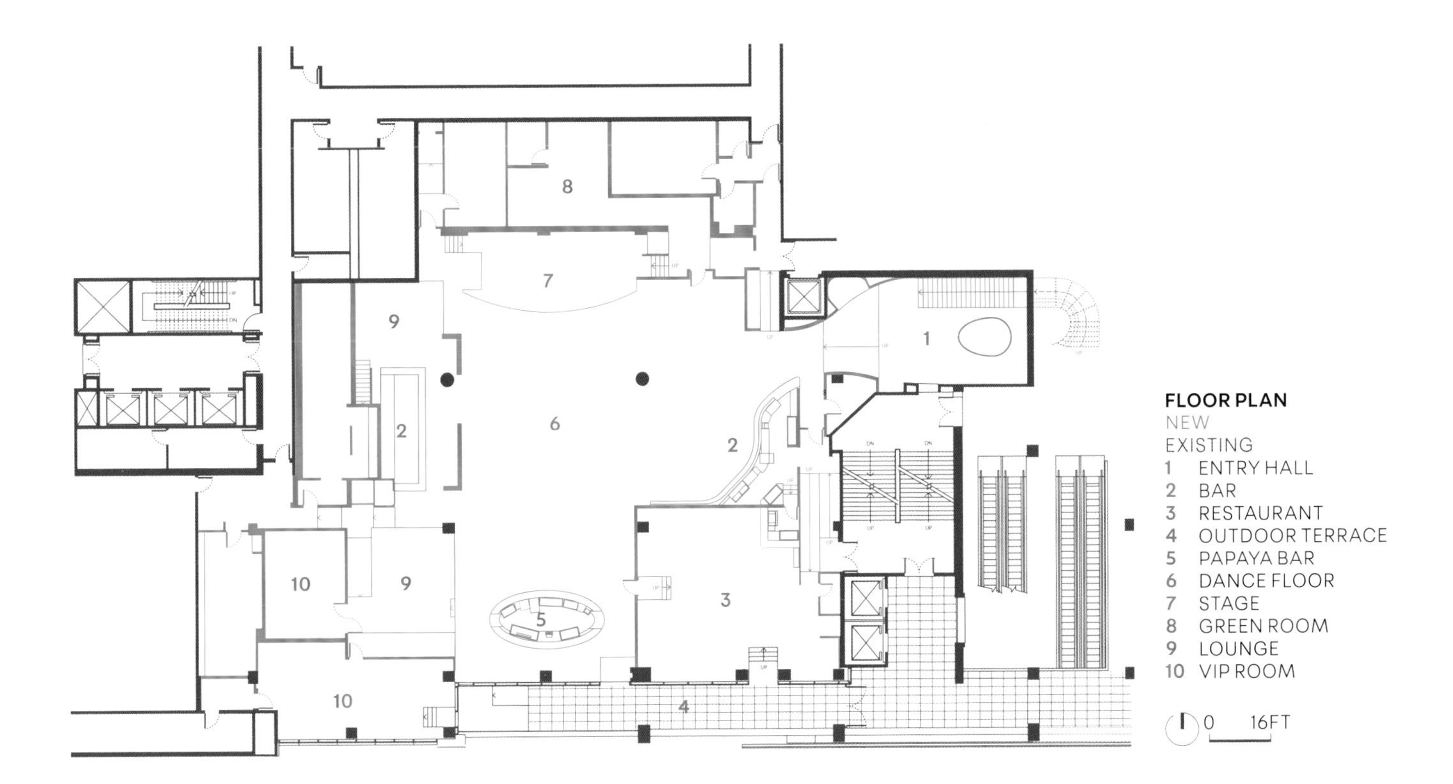

Conga Room at L.A. Live

LOS ANGELES, CALIFORNIA, U.S.A.
2007–2008

The Conga Room is a Los Angeles institution known for its live Latin music and dancing. This iteration of the venue was part of the city's downtown revitalization and is situated in a second-floor unit originally planned as office space. The 14,000-square-foot project uses a unifying motif to both draw patrons upstairs to explore the Conga Room's various enclaves and support the state-of-the-art audio-visual system.

The experience of the space begins at the street level with a 20-foot-tall acrylic "tornado" that hangs from the second floor and peeks through an opening carved out of the concrete slab. This initial visual attractor rises to the ceiling above and morphs into an undulating pattern of medium-density fiberboard (MDF) panels that proliferate throughout, guiding users deeper into the venue. The panels form six-petal "flowers" angled to help acoustically isolate and absorb sound; they also camouflage utilities in the ceiling such as sprinklers, speakers, and security cameras, and reflect the lighting programming. This motif works in concert with contributions from Cuban American artist Jorge Pardo, who designed one of the three distinct bars, and Mexican performer and muralist Sergio Arau, which, together, form a cohesive environment with custom spatial cues floating above the sea of revelers.

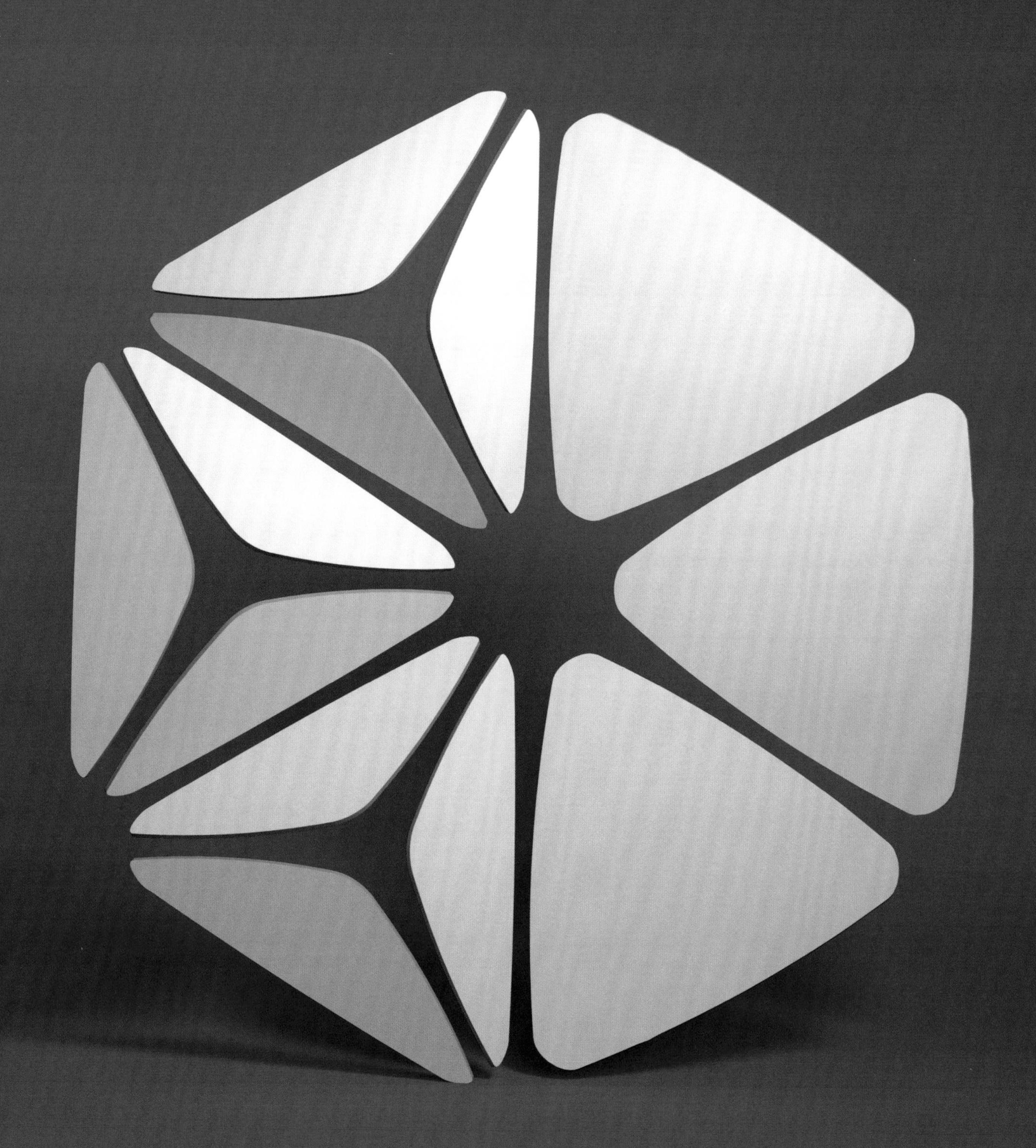

CEILING CONSTRUCTION

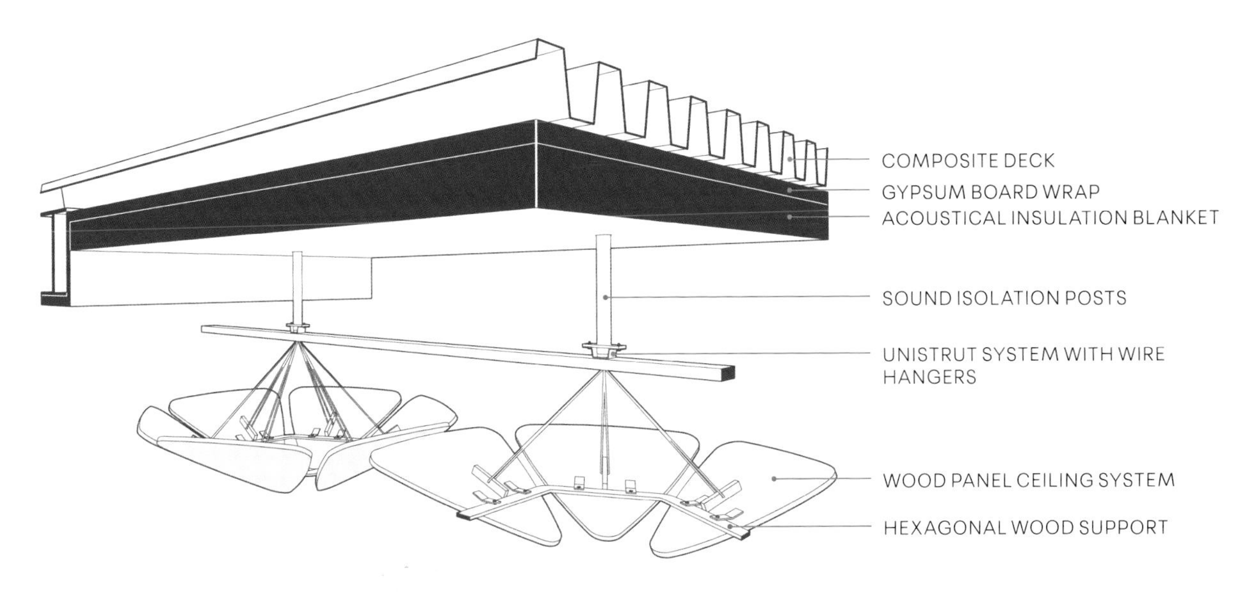

FLOWER ELEVATION

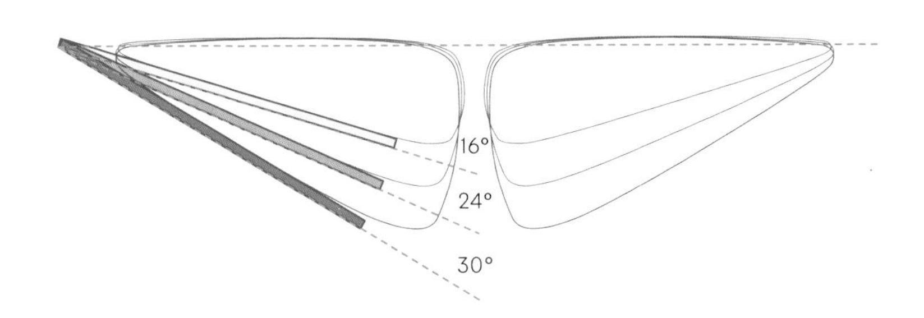

REFLECTED CEILING PLAN

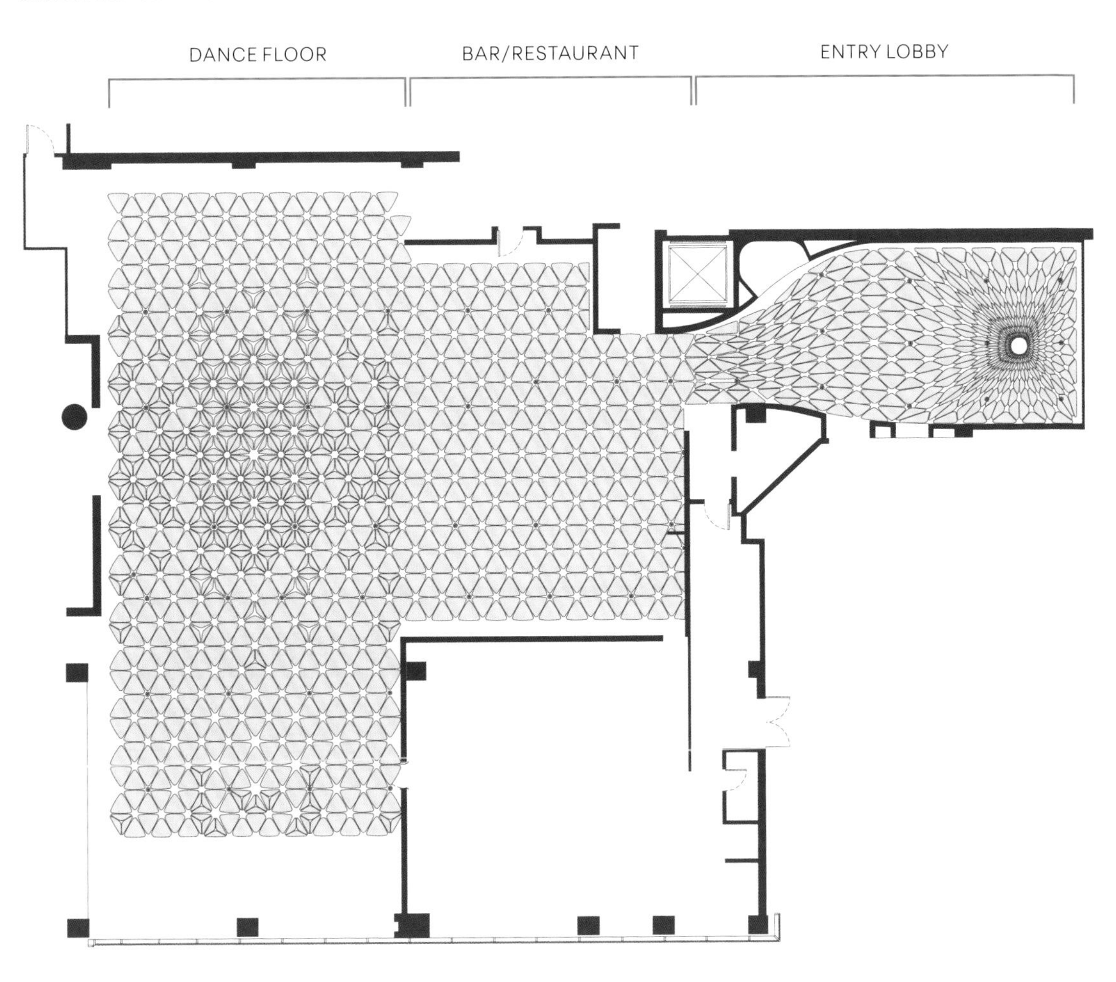

The articulated "flowers" transform based on the location and function of the space beneath them. They are variegated to allow for light and sound dispersal, while also differentiating active and passive spaces.

TORNADO CONSTRUCTION

1 UNISTRUT
2 RIBS
3 CABLES
4 PETALS
5 RINGS

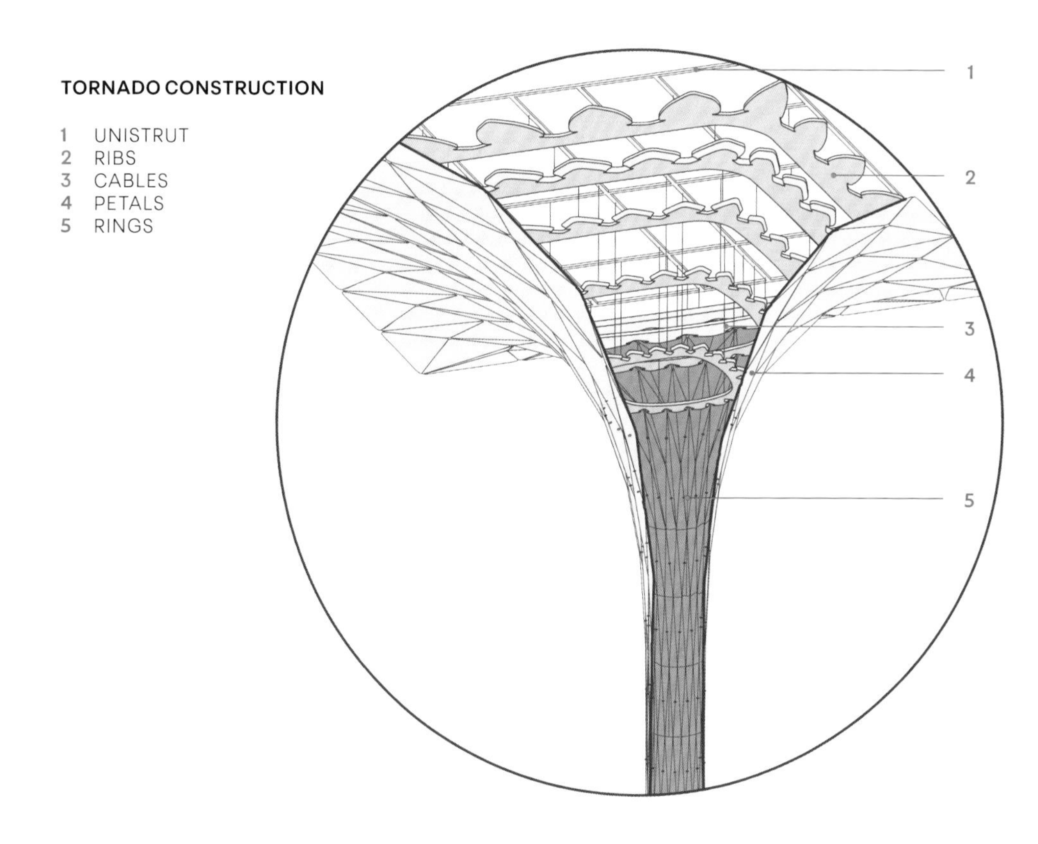

BELOW AND OPPOSITE: As a visitor enters the venue on the lower level, the ceiling panels merge and descend into a 20-foot-tall acrylic "tornado," defining the dramatic unfolding of the space beyond.

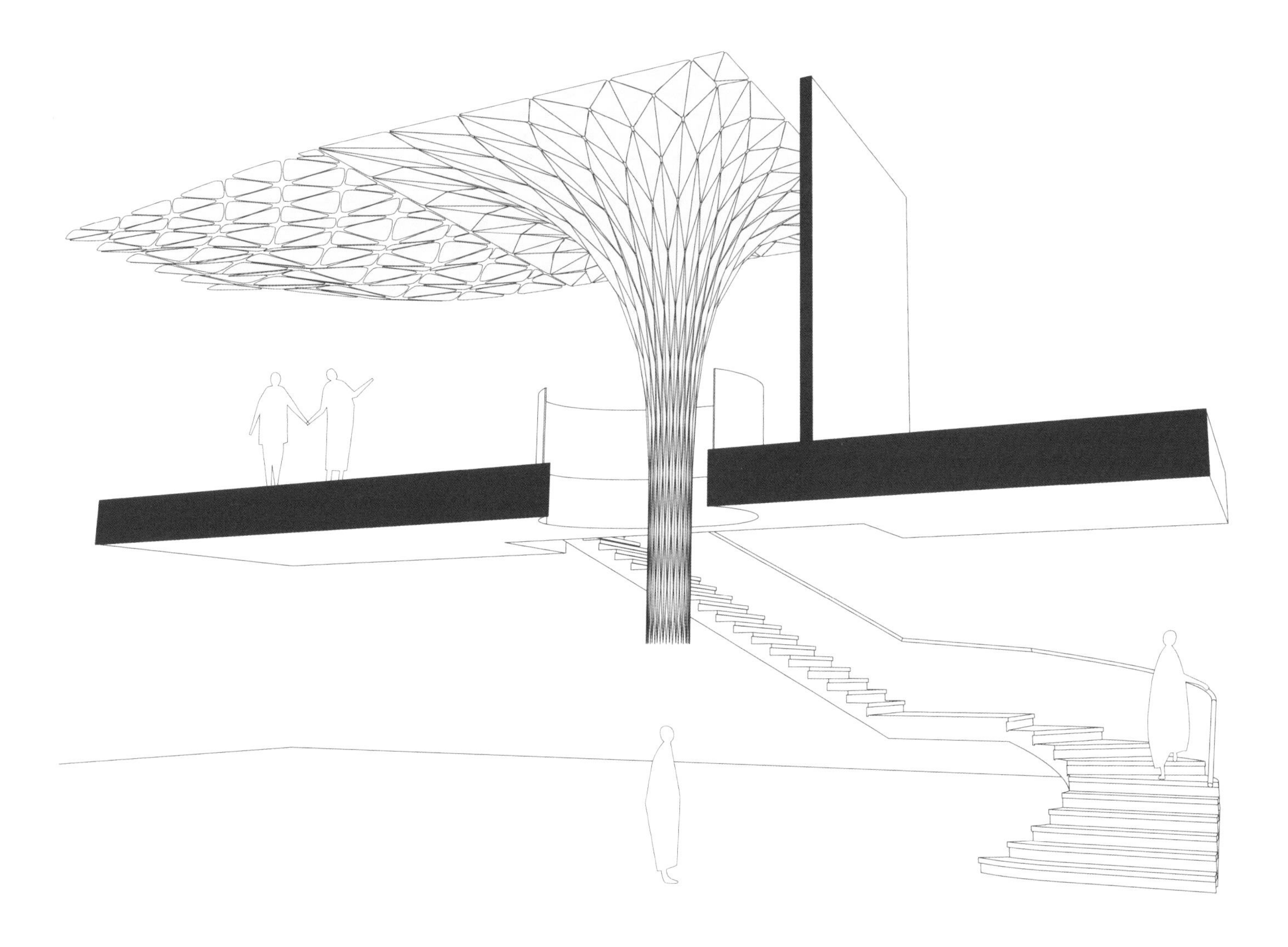

The integrated ceiling system descends into a custom floor opening, providing light and connectivity to the lower lobby.

Nokia 5300 XpressMusic

OPPOSITE, ABOVE, AND FOLLOWING PAGES:
The bar, lounge, and dance floor area are integrated as a cohesive experience of pattern, color, and light.

4

PREVIOUS PAGES: The innovative yet practical use of shotcrete for the Holocaust Museum LA allowed for sculptural and expressive concrete forms.

ABOVE AND OPPOSITE: The surface of Pan Pacific Park is conceptually lifted, with the museum tucked below.

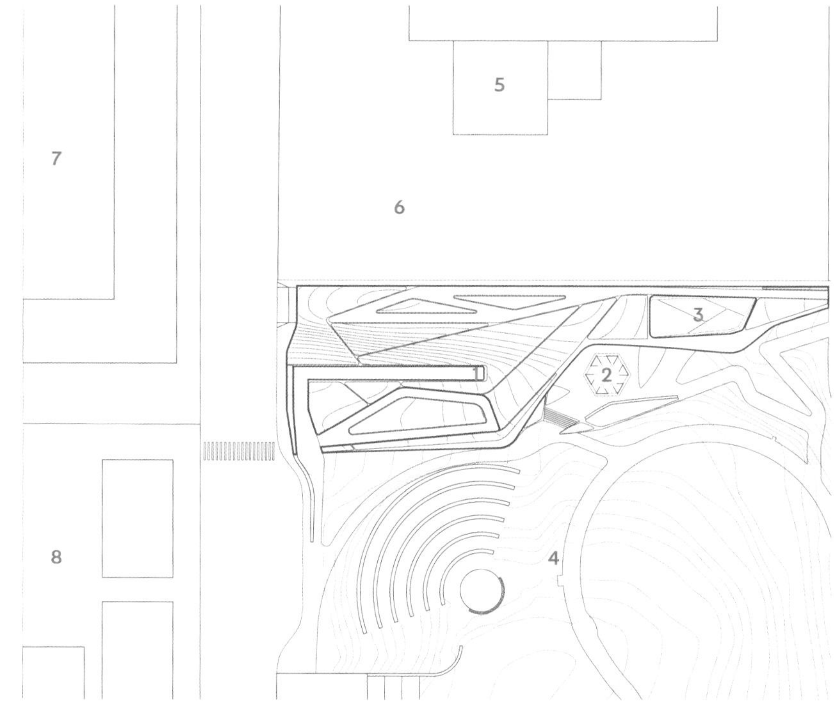

SITE PLAN
1 MUSEUM
2 EXISTING HOLOCAUST MEMORIAL
3 CHILDREN'S MEMORIAL
4 PAN PACIFIC PARK
5 UNITED STATES POSTAL SERVICE (USPS)
6 USPS PARKING
7 RESIDENTIAL COMPLEX
8 CBS STUDIOS

Holocaust Museum LA (formerly Los Angeles Museum of the Holocaust)

LOS ANGELES, CALIFORNIA, U.S.A.
2004–2010

Holocaust Museum LA (formerly Los Angeles Museum of the Holocaust) is embedded in the landscape of Pan Pacific Park, obscuring the mass of the building while bringing new life to the area. At the time of its design and construction, the museum became an early exemplar of parametric design and has since remained an enduring architectural landmark in the city.

The experience of the 32,000-square-foot museum is defined by stark contrasts that serve as meditative cues for patrons descending into the building: above versus below ground, light and darkness, planted landscape juxtaposed with raw concrete, and ambient noise from the park dampened by the hush of the galleries. Together, these dichotomies create an inextricable link between the design narrative and the project's form, priming visitors for the impact of the exhibitions within.

Sustainability has been integral to the building's design. The subterranean project features one of the largest intensive green roofs in California, which acts as insulation and limits exposure to the elements. Pervious paving and the slope of the site increase the efficiency of groundwater collection in cisterns below, which is then used to irrigate the landscape above. In addition, the concrete throughout was primarily mixed with fly ash, an eco-friendly material, and left raw. The project has been certified LEED Gold and has maintained a symbiosis with the surrounding landscape.

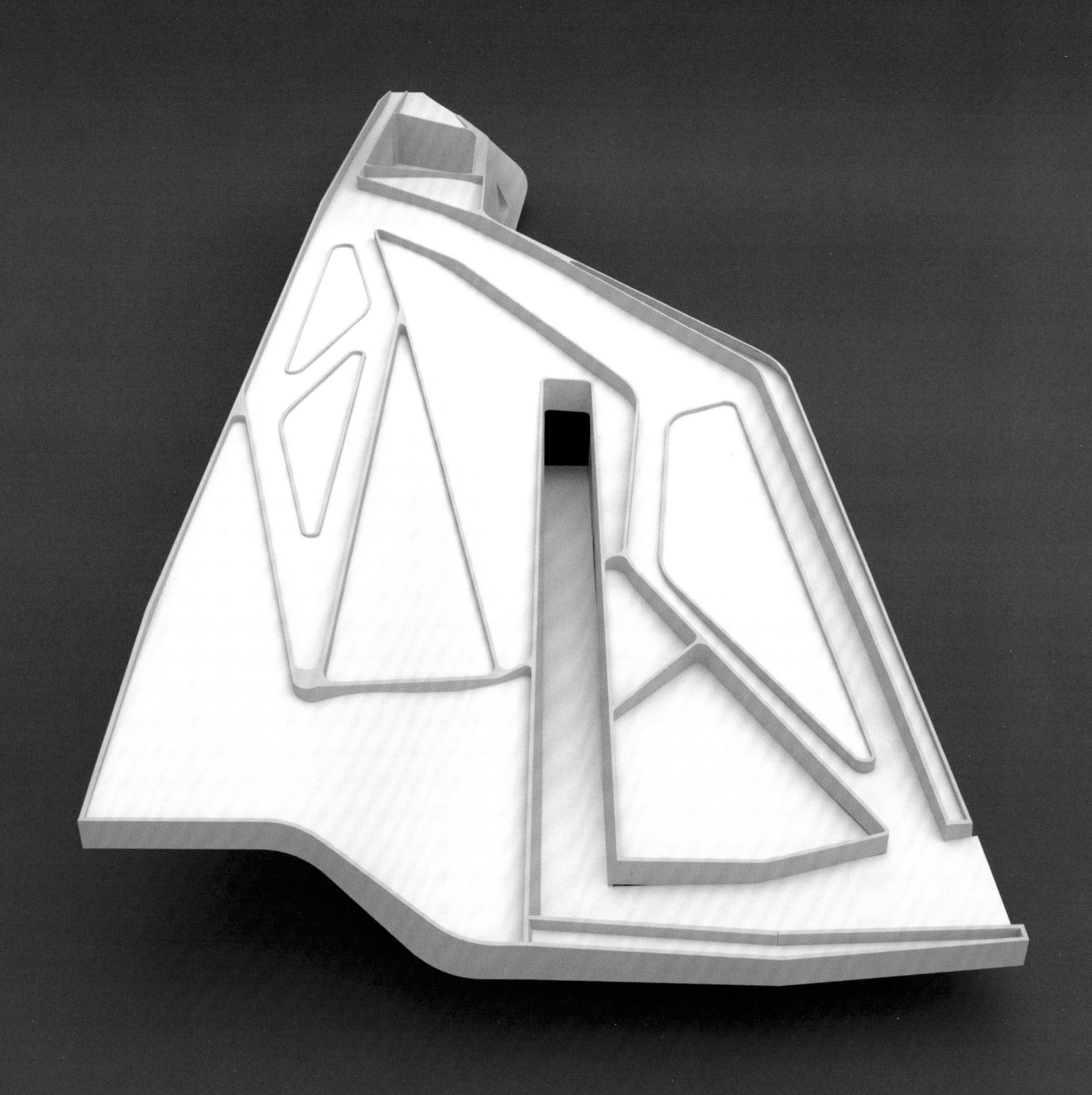

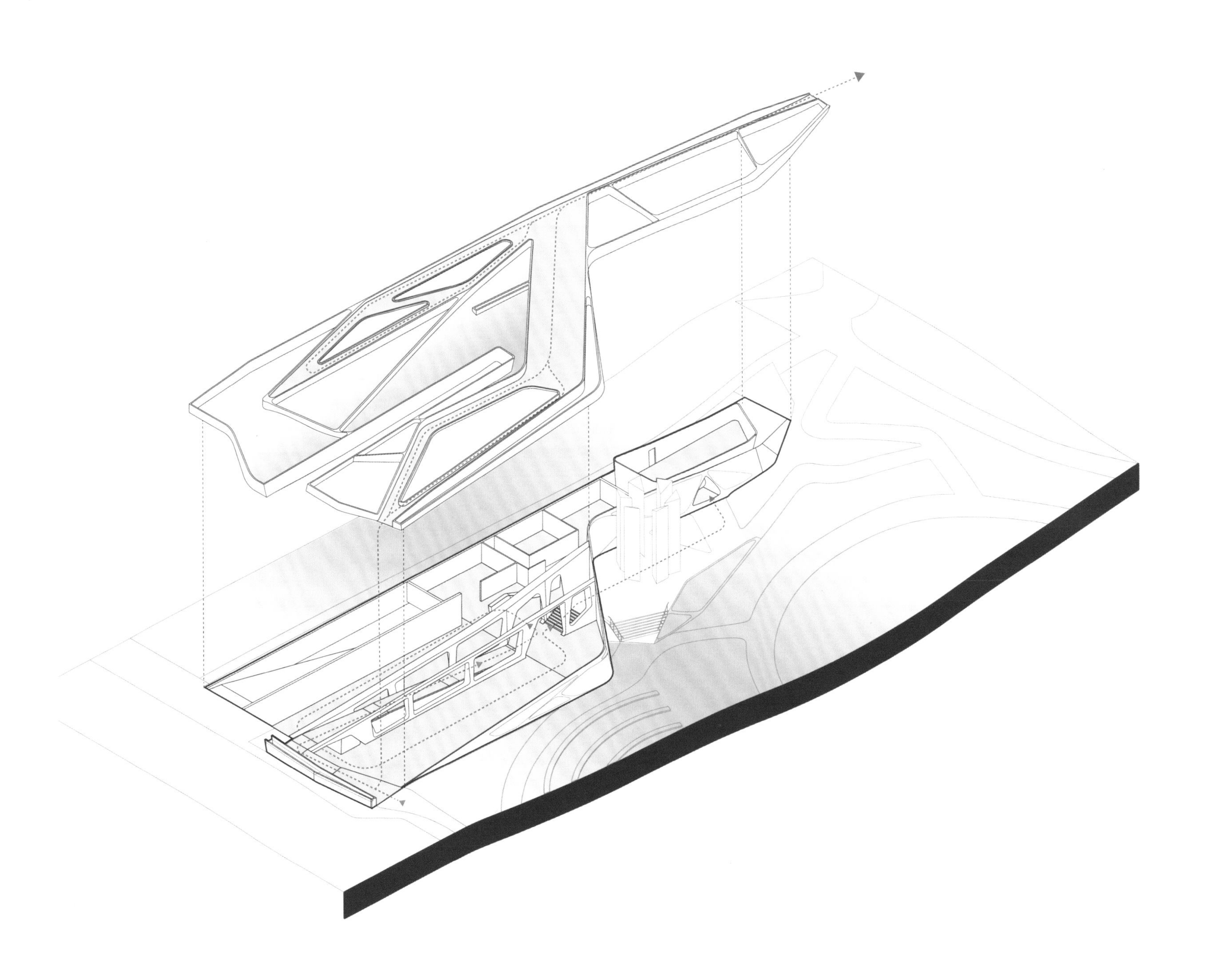

The museum's circulation path guides visitors on a gradual descent below the landscape and through a chronological experience of the Holocaust.

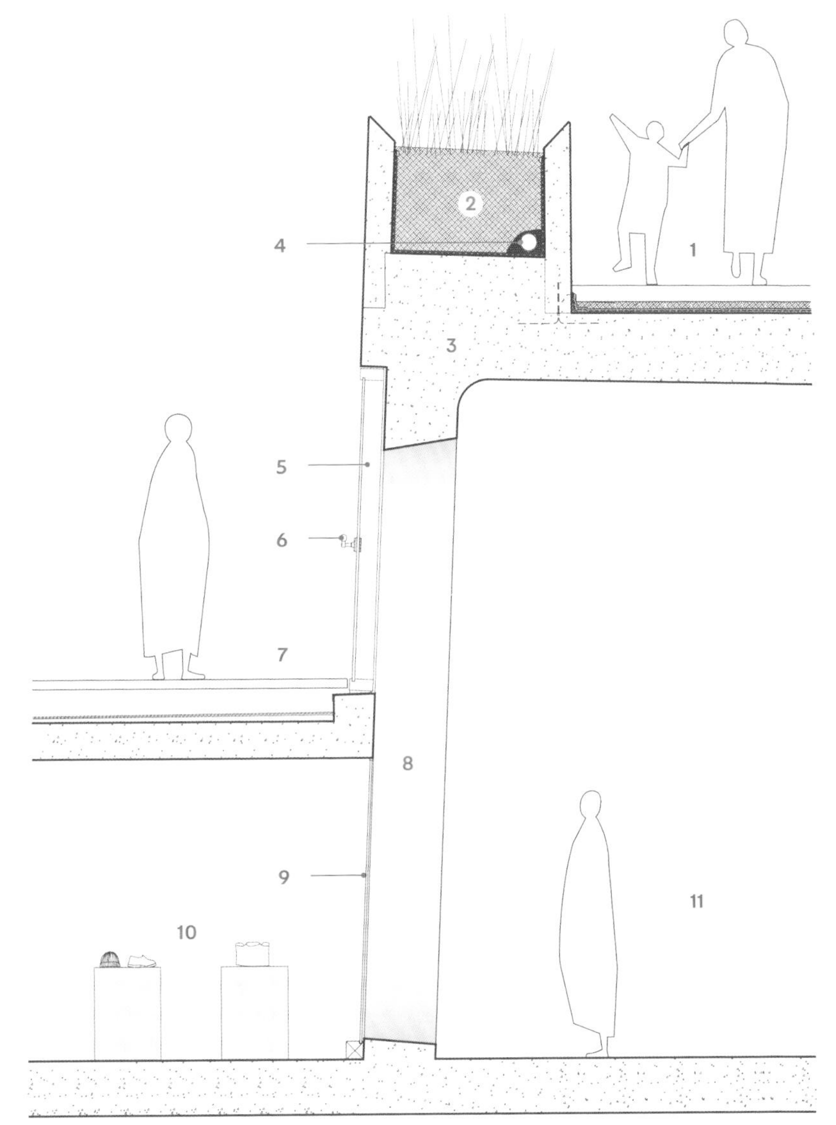

PARTIAL ENTRANCE RAMP SECTION
1 WALKING PATH
2 DROUGHT-TOLERANT PLANTING
3 POURED-IN-PLACE CONCRETE
4 FRENCH DRAIN
5 STOREFRONT GLAZING
6 HANDRAIL
7 OPEN CONCRETE PAVER
8 SCULPTED CONCRETE OPENING
9 FIXED GLAZING
10 ARTIFACT DISPLAY CASE
11 GALLERY

OPPOSITE: The central defining element of the museum, the ramp is bookended by translucent glazing that tapers to evoke a sense of gradual descent and departure from the world above.

ABOVE: Internally, the ramp divides the gallery both vertically and horizontally; beneath it is a humidity- and temperature-controlled exhibition space for the display of sensitive artifacts.

FAR LEFT: Extensive formwork for the ramp walls created a continuous surface for the fly-ash concrete (LEFT) to be applied.

LEFT AND BELOW: Craftsmen specializing in swimming pool construction used two-dimensional stencils to shape the ruled-surface concrete forms.

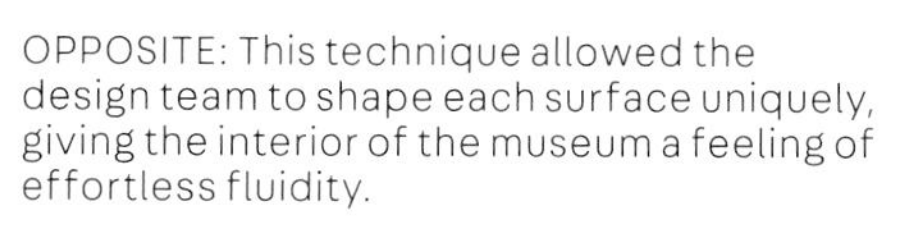

OPPOSITE: This technique allowed the design team to shape each surface uniquely, giving the interior of the museum a feeling of effortless fluidity.

PREVIOUS PAGES: The entry ramp, which provides the primary source of natural light, naturally tapers, making the space gradually darker and lighter in concert with the chronology and contents of the exhibits.

The entry door (ABOVE) and lobby area (OPPOSITE) are framed with elegantly sculptural concrete work.

FOUNDATION ATRIUM

185
PERSECUTIONS

OPPOSITE: Technology is used to teach students and visitors. The interactive table offers opportunities for students to connect with the content and learn more about individual Holocaust victims, survivors, and their stories.

ABOVE: At the lowest point in the elevation of the museum, there is no natural light. Visitors find their way via large, backlit images of the darkest period of the Holocaust—the architecture amplifies the content.

ABOVE: Bespoke kiosks, each representing a different major death camp, are placed at the lowest and darkest space in the museum.

OPPOSITE: Small gathering areas offer a space for visitors to listen to survivor talks—a critical component to expanding the museum's message.

FOLLOWING PAGES: The grass-covered roof is an extension of the park and its pathways.

FLUID DYNAMICS
Sarah Amelar

High above the desks at Belzberg Architects' studio in Santa Monica, California, a veiling layer hovers just beneath the ceiling. Like a halo over the drafting room, it turns out to be an element from the firm's work elsewhere: the same acoustical product it transformed in various ways throughout its interiors for the USC Shoah Foundation. And punctuating the studio walls are other specimens from its research and experimentation, including a full-size mock-up for windows at the Gores Group Headquarters, with slumped glass billowing out like a giant swatch of bubble wrap. There's also a drawing for that building's flat roof canopy—a two-dimensional web of wireframe-modeled lines that appears as undulant as a topographic relief map. In a sense, this workspace is a lab, an incubator for ideas, and it becomes clear that each project is a new investigation.

Yet, as wide-ranging as these abundant explorations seem in material and form, they have common threads. One theme that emerges again and again, morphing as it goes, is the evocation of dynamic flow patterns—surging and ebbing—throughout the body of work. In the Los Angeles restaurant Patina and Disney Concert Hall, as well as the Ahmanson Founders Room at the city's Music Center, that sense of motion seems to ripple through the deep, wood panels that line walls and ceilings, or, like a massive drape, divide spaces. By contrast, in some of the firm's other explorations, the material joints themselves become expressive, suggesting converging and diverging lines of force—as in the luminous, glass media wall at Occidental College's McKinnon Center for Global Affairs or the concrete cladding of the Pavilion at City of Hope. While all evoke flux, each of these solutions is project-specific, resolving multiple challenges simultaneously, from the practical to the metaphoric.

At City of Hope, a research and treatment center for cancer and other life-threatening diseases, in Duarte, California, the expression of fluidity goes well beyond elevating the emotive and experiential qualities of this hospital-and-laboratory compound—it plays a role in clarifying the logic of the entire campus. Here, Belzberg Architects' intimate meeting-exhibition venue acknowledges the rectilinear character of City of Hope's existing buildings by integrating that trait while also expressively reinterpreting and tempering it. At the core of the solution is the way the pavilion, composed of two small buildings, defines and embraces the space around a majestic tree: a century-old camphor with an enormous canopy. Standing at the nexus of treatment and research zones, the great

tree—as framed by this project's low structures—becomes an organizing and meditative focal point for the whole complex. That gesture is further intensified by the visual fluidity of the pavilion's forms and the animated joint lines across them. While the backs of these modest concrete-clad structures, oriented toward the rest of campus, appear as straight-edged and gridded as the surrounding buildings, the new architecture departs from the orthogonal where it faces the tree, curving as if melding into softer volumes. And with that deformation around the camphor, the lines incised across the concrete (and accentuated by points of light) deflect, as if registering energy fields emitted by the monumental tree.

As organic and compelling as this fusion of siting and allusive fluidity may seem, this was actually not the location the client originally had in mind. The initial plan was to renovate an existing bungalow, but Hagy Belzberg intuitively gravitated toward the tree. And, as he and his client learned much later, it embodied an unexpectedly fitting symbol for City of Hope. Camphor is an ancient Asian species with medicinal uses and a well-earned reputation for resiliency and longevity. (It was one of the first life forms to recover from the devastation by atomic bombings in Japan, sprouting back far sooner than anticipated and with remarkable vigor.) The focus on this particular camphor brought the work an added twist of synchronicity: the pavilion commemorates City of Hope's one-hundredth anniversary—making the institution the exact same age as this now-celebrated tree.

Much the way this small-scale project engages in dialogue with the larger context, the pavilion's interior plays off its exterior. Inside, the architects transformed the simple box of a conference room, in part, with a trompe l'oeil ceiling that evokes contours, fluidity, and depth. They achieved this effect with a stretched polyvinyl membrane, a material more typically used in malls for economical backlit signage and other displays, so custom printing was a standard option. But, unlike the attention-grabbing graphics often associated with this product, the complex, fine-lined pattern the design team devised gives the room a nuanced, hovering terrain overhead and a feeling of expansive height without being distracting. Also, because this material was originally developed commercially for rear illumination, it performs a diffusing role here, veiling light fixtures (along with any infrastructure) above it.

ABOVE: A century-old camphor tree is a natural contrast to the grid-deformed shotcrete wall on the campus of the Pavilion at City of Hope.

The Pavilion at City of Hope (ABOVE TOP) and the Conga Room at L.A. Live (ABOVE BOTTOM) are contrasting examples of depth of surface treatments—in flat graphic pattern and in three dimensions, respectively.

The play of depth and texture, achieved through the repurposing or metamorphosis of inexpensive, readily available products and methods, recurs throughout the firm's work. At the Patina restaurant and Ahmanson Founders Room, for example, the highly sculptural wood panels are computer numerical control (CNC)-carved composites of standard glued laminated (glulam) beams, and, at the USC Shoah Foundation, digital routing gives unique, character-altering textures to an off-the-shelf, sound-buffering material, fabricated from recycled plastics.

For the Conga Room, a Latin nightclub at L.A. Live, the firm adapted other everyday materials both for dramatic effect and the resolution of spatial and logistical obstacles. The challenges behind this interiors project were significant: the existing shell had the mundane proportions of office space, and key club areas needed to occupy an upper level, one story above grade, where few customers would naturally gravitate. Adding to that, the dense crowds that fill a successful club of this type tend to obscure any coherent reading of floor or wall decor. And from a purely practical standpoint, acoustic and motion isolation were essential—as was a vast web of back-of-the-house components, including sound and lighting systems, that needed to be hidden from view but accessible to staff throughout the Conga Room. In exploring these issues, the architects soon realized that the ceiling offered the one plane that could remain visible and unobstructed across the club. So, they created vivid patterns overhead to guide the stream of patrons—even leading them upstairs.

Drawing on compositions derived from Latin textiles and flowers (and working in collaboration with artists—Cuban-American Jorge Pardo and Mexican Sergio Arau—on parts of the project), the architects developed a dynamic three-dimensional surface of clipped-in and cost-effective medium-density fiberboard (MDF) plates, illuminated by color- and mood-altering LED lights. This energized ceiling—with plenty of opportunities to tuck away isolators and networks while leaving ports accessible—reinforces spatial continuity and generates that sense of motion calibrated to promote the flow of people. The exuberant patterning culminates in a pendant, tornado-like form that doubles as a chandelier: a visual magnet that descends within the winding staircase to the upper level. Offering glimpses up to the floor above, the stairway beckons patrons to ascend. So, this radical rethinking of surfaces, tying together the many components of this club, becomes spatially, functionally, and experientially transformative.

At Apertures, a new six-story building in Mexico City, which will house a hotel, spec office space, a restaurant, and a subterranean parking garage, the constraints and opportunities were quite different. Here, exterior sun shading and earthquake resiliency were key concerns. Additionally, the architects were committed to working with local resources and methods, as well as elements of the region's deep-rooted language of built form.

With its solution, the Belzberg team adapted traditional means to create sweeping exterior brise-soleils—triangular "sails" that wrap the structure's glass curtain walls and projecting balconies. Composed of polymerized concrete masonry units, the veil takes Mexico's ubiquitous breeze-block sunscreens, literally and figuratively, to greater heights—spanning the building's six stories, bowing out with complex curves, and appearing animated by an implicit suggestion of windblown motion. While integrating earthquake protections into this outer sheath, the firm devised an innovative structural system that is easy and economical to fabricate and construct. Yet those practical achievements are inextricable from the design's dialogue with the local vernacular and the resulting dramatic gesture.

Through marrying a familiar building feature with seismic performance, the architects produced a system, composed of relatively lightweight masonry units, that significantly enhances both the structural and expressive capabilities of the breeze wall. Invisibly joining the blocks are C-shaped steel plates, each inserted neatly into a cast recess in both of the adjoining masonry units and bolted together there with only two nuts. Collectively behaving as slender "columns," the plates fasten together in continuous, curving vertical lines (connected at either end to a perimeter steel frame), thereby eliminating the need for grout, mortar, or rebar. This system also allows the entire wall of blocks to flex like a single mesh under lateral forces.

The minimal, yet highly effective, hardware connections belong to the kit of parts that the firm developed for precision and simplicity in both fabrication and assembly. Bolt holes in each numbered block ensure the specific offset and placement of every masonry unit to produce continuous curves. With an economy of means, the process required only two unique molds, modified with minor inserts to achieve a rich textural variation that invites the play of light and shadow. Each masonry unit is channel-like, revealing a large, angled, or faceted, void within. Such a

At Apertures, a tectonic, aggregative masonry block system is embedded within an entirely different language of continuity and sweeping curvilinear surfaces.

significant degree of openness—made possible by the strength of the overall ensemble—allows the entire screen to be more transparent (or glowing, when lit from within by night).

As in most of the practice's work, the results are simultaneously novel and familiar, complex and simple. Back in the studio, an up-close look at a prototype block for Apertures makes the clarity of that solution tangible. The unit feels even lighter than anticipated, and its metal fitting is remarkably uncomplicated and compact. Beyond that, the actual artifact, examined at close range, begins to reveal the experimental processes that enabled the designers to make expanses of concrete masonry block billow. It's a feat akin—in spirit, rather than material or form—to the wavelets that seemingly course through the thick wood panels at Ahmanson and Patina, or the implicit lines of force that appear to deflect concrete at City of Hope or expanses of glass at Occidental College. Across Belzberg Architects' portfolio, many such solutions emerge, sending out ripples or streams that they will most likely reroute or reinterpret in the work to come—allowing the concepts to flow with the specifics of place and circumstance, obstacles and opportunities.

The large glass interactive display at the McKinnon Center for Global Affairs at Occidental College overlays dynamic form and light effects with information graphics.

Tropical Ecology in Costa Rica
Trade Impacts
Now Playing: Map of Dispatches; Student Life
Map of Dispatches
Dance Production 2013
RAW Records
Global Crossroads
Global Crossroads
Dance Production 2013

Kona Residence

KONA, HAWAII, U.S.A.
2006–2010

The Kona Residence merges with the unique character of its site, blurring the distinction between the architectural intervention and the existing landscape. Located on the west coast of Hawaii's Big Island, views to dormant volcanoes Mauna Kea and Hualālai to the east and southeast, respectively, and to the ocean to the west informed the skewed orientation of the house established by the project's main axis. This circulation spine is an open-air corridor that provides a well-traversed gallery for the owner's orchid collection and an unobstructed view of the landscape beyond. The rest of the program is distributed in pods off this thoroughfare, each with sleeping quarters and adjacent common areas that connect to the surroundings with carefully orchestrated vistas. Overall, the layout maintains an openness to the landscape at every turn.

The house is positioned between exposed, cooled lava flows, juxtaposing geometric architectural forms with lush greenery and an amorphous black landscape. The building's material palette echoes this context, including stacked and cut lava rock and reclaimed teak timber from old barns for the exterior of the home; the pool, which meets the exposed lava flows at its foot, has also been capped with cut lava and its black porcelain basin selected to match. Overall, the residence emphasizes the connection between built form and the island's natural conditions, suggesting the former's low profile has emerged from the latter as an extension of the island's form.

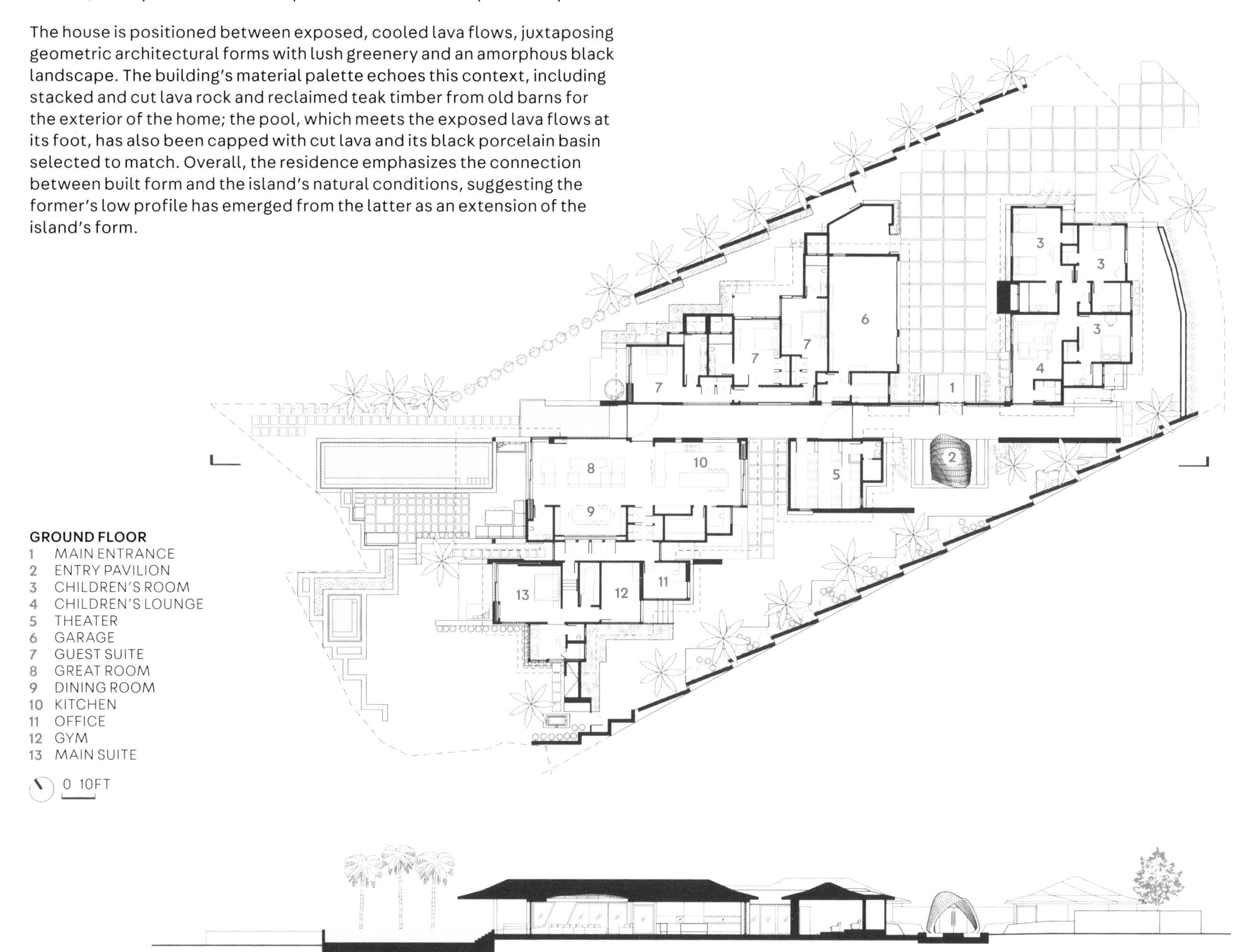

PREVIOUS PAGES: The stacked stone walls gently descend to create framed interiors.

ABOVE: A reflecting pool at the end of the exterior gallery takes in the Hawaiian sunset.

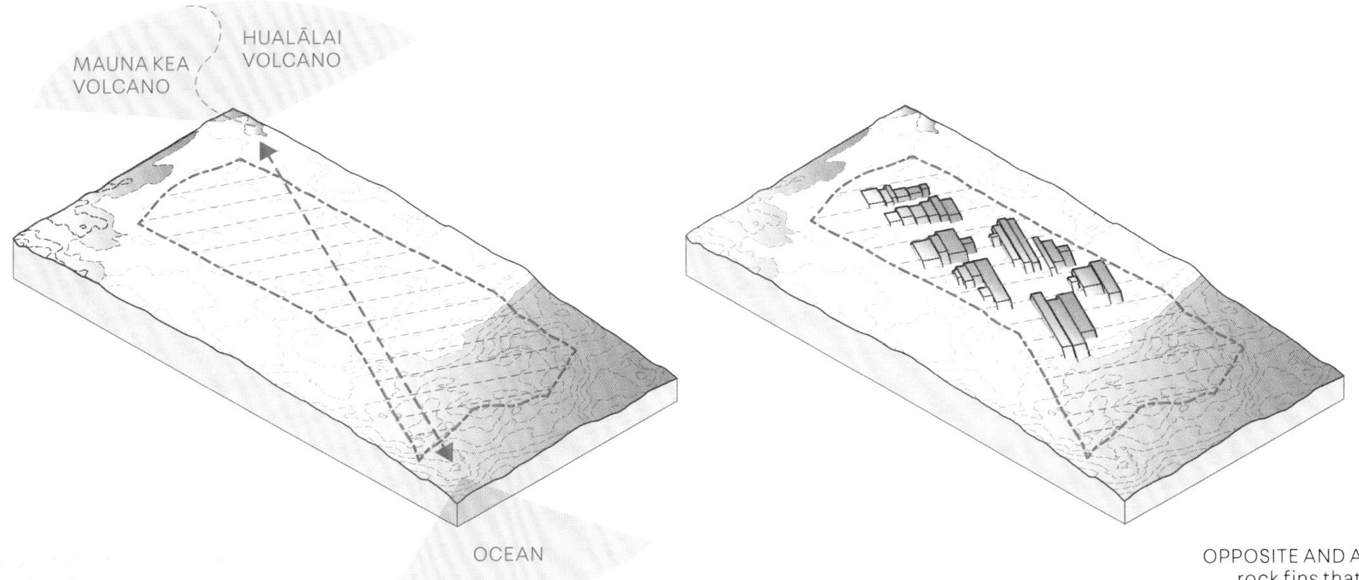

OPPOSITE AND ABOVE RIGHT: A series of lava rock fins that emerge from the landscape dictates the structural concept.

ABOVE LEFT AND BELOW: The project's oblique site orientation within the natural lava flow maximizes views of the two volcanoes to the east, and the Pacific Ocean to the west.

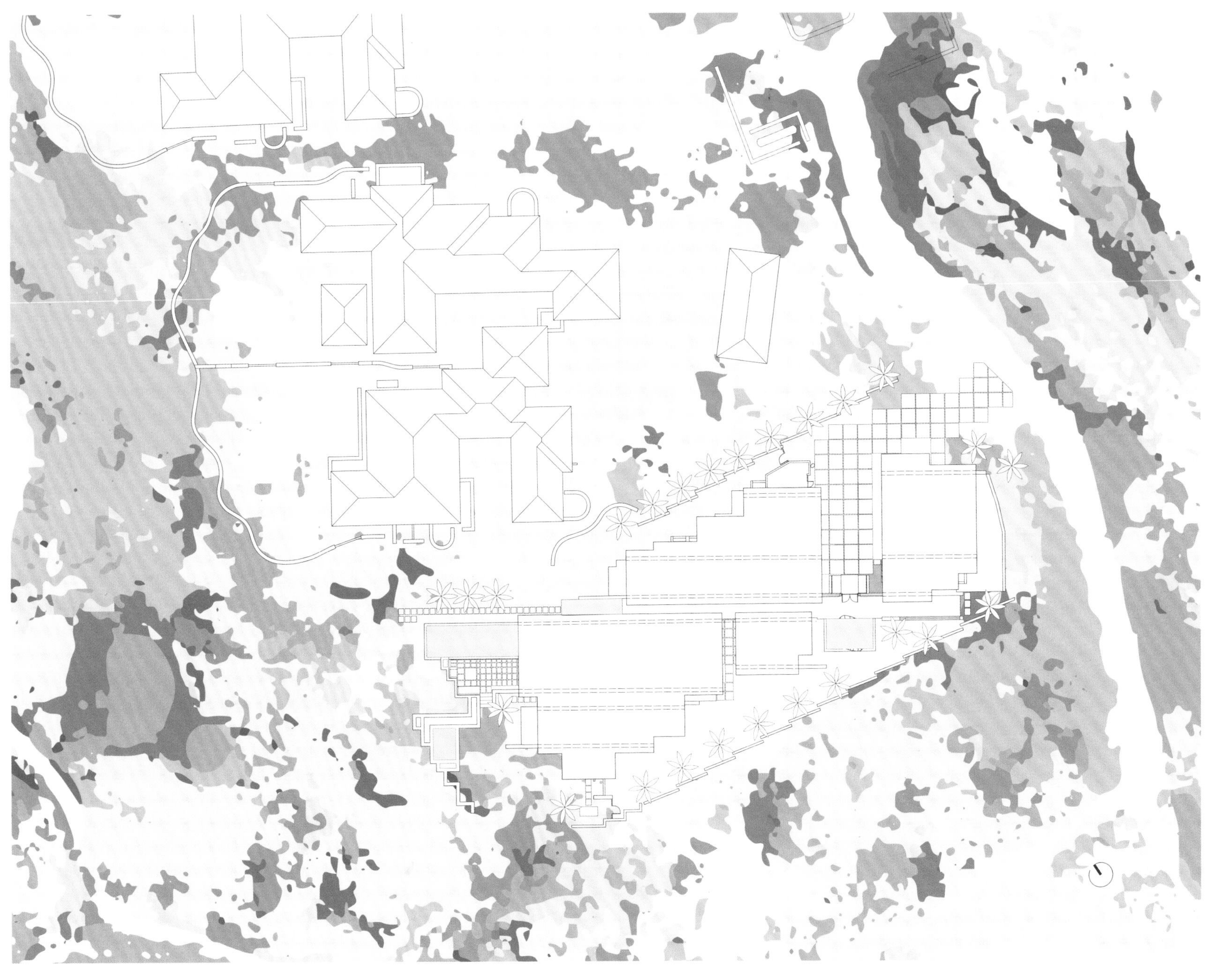

ABOVE: The entry sequence along the open-air circulation spine features some of the more unique design elements. A sculptural gazebo consisting of prefabricated, marine-grade plywood panels greets visitors at the entry pavilion.

OPPOSITE: A series of bespoke stainless steel armatures holding conic glass vases displays the owner's orchid collection.

ABOVE: Corner-opening pocket doors frame the view from the main bedroom to the Pacific Ocean. Bespoke carved wood finishes evoke the integral Hawaiian heritage.

OPPOSITE: An elevated infinity pool extends into the lanai, eroding the line between indoors and outdoors.

FOLLOWING PAGES: The swimming pool harvests the color of the sky.

6

McKinnon Center for Global Affairs at Occidental College

LOS ANGELES, CALIFORNIA, U.S.A.
2010–2013

The renovation of the McKinnon Center for Global Affairs simultaneously revitalized the historic elements of the existing building and applied a contemporary approach to pedagogy in reconfiguring the learning environment. The result is an immersive experience that encourages engagement and cross-pollination across the center's community, both in-person and online.

At the McKinnon Center, learning is done out in the open. New flexible breakout spaces have been added throughout, and classrooms are reduced in size to encourage informal peer-to-peer study in corridors facilitated by the addition of whiteboard walls and benches. The Global Forum, a custom web application for students, faculty, and administrators to author and publish multimedia projects for display to their peers and guests, has also been developed in collaboration with the college and an interdisciplinary design team. The forum's physical manifestation—a new backlit, two-story media wall comprising screens embedded in custom, panelized, slumped glass—livestreams information and content from the online platform, allowing everyone to see and participate in the big ideas and thought-provoking discussions that motivate courses and events at the center.

The exemplar of the seamless integration of old and new is the transformation of the lecture theater. Built as a chapel, the restoration highlights the beauty of the room's original features including the windows and crafted-wood beams in the ceiling. In contrast, dark computer numerical control (CNC)-cut acoustic paneling with a curvaceous pattern has been installed to address a functional need without distracting from the historic elements. Seating is now rotated, maintaining the 170 count, but allowing lecturers to be closer to the audience, while new breakout areas in the upper wings support greater engagement and visual connection as desired. Here, equal value has been given to the institution's history and its future.

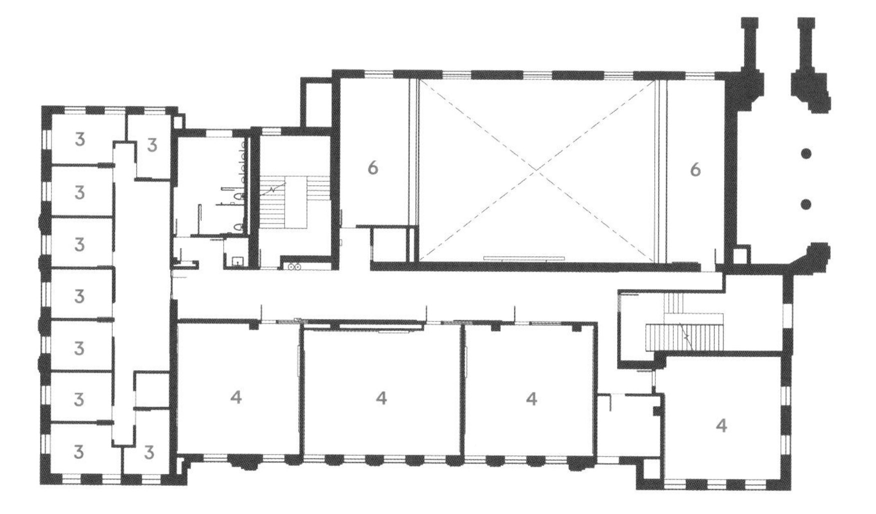

THIRD FLOOR

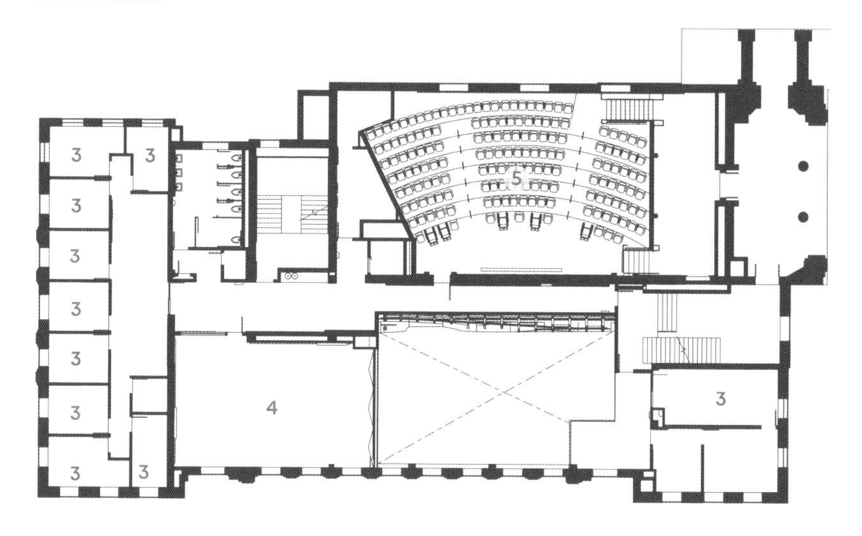

SECOND FLOOR

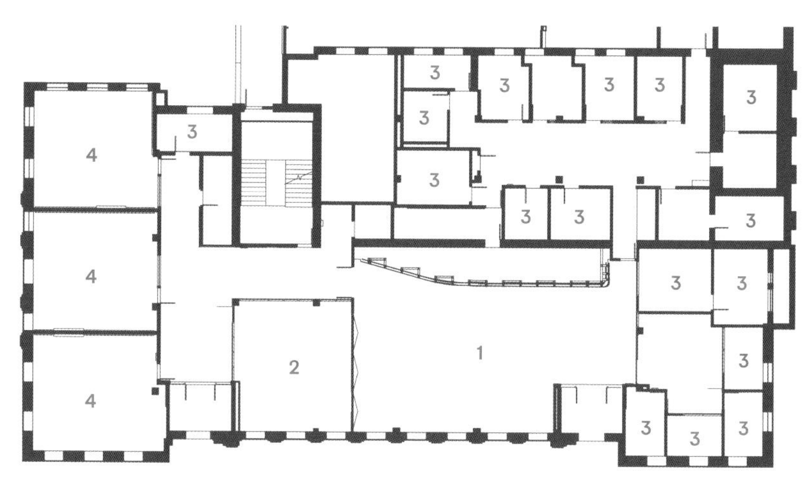

GROUND FLOOR

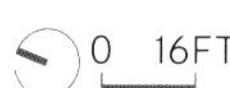

FLOOR PLANS AND SECTION

1 MEDIA WALL AND LOBBY
2 INNOVATION LAB
3 OFFICE
4 CLASSROOM
5 AUDITORIUM
6 BALCONY

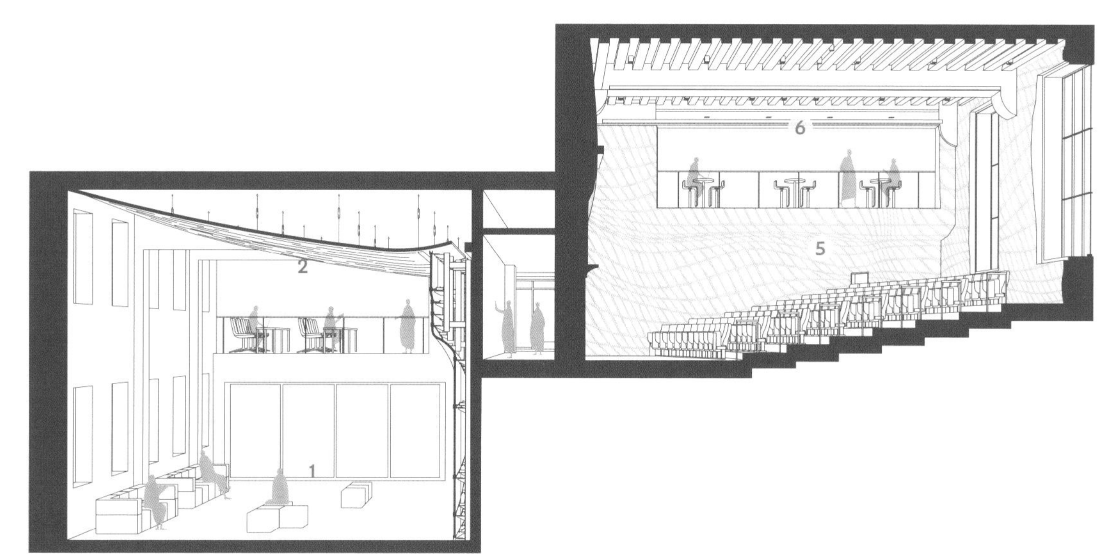

PREVIOUS PAGES: The original wood windows and painted wood ceilings in the McKinnon Center for Global Affairs' Choi Auditorium were left uncovered during the renovation.

ABOVE: An interactive classroom features operable windows that overlook the Global Forum media wall and lobby.

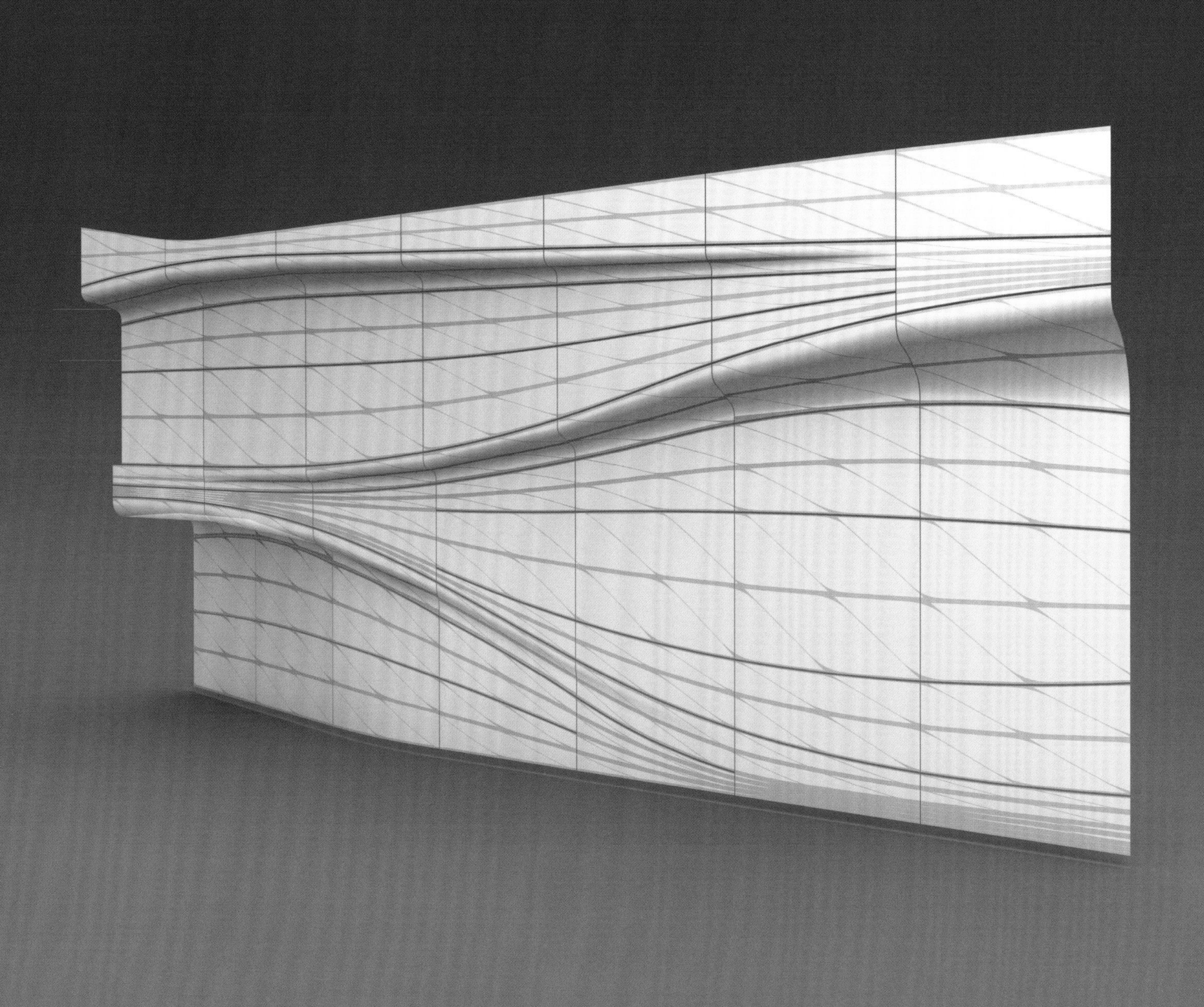

CLASSROOM CIRCULATION

EXISTING

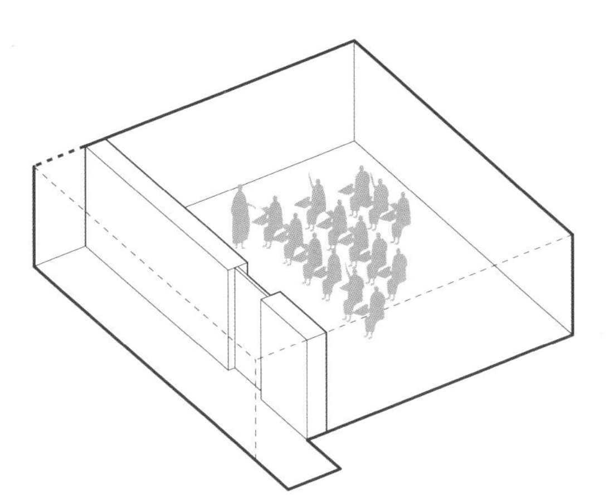

OPPOSITE: The double-height media wall in the lobby is sculpted in a pattern evoking an immersive fluidity.

LEFT: The second-floor circulation space has been widened and furnished with whiteboard walls and benches to encourage informal interactions between students and faculty.

Hands

MEDIA WALL AND LOBBY
EXISTING

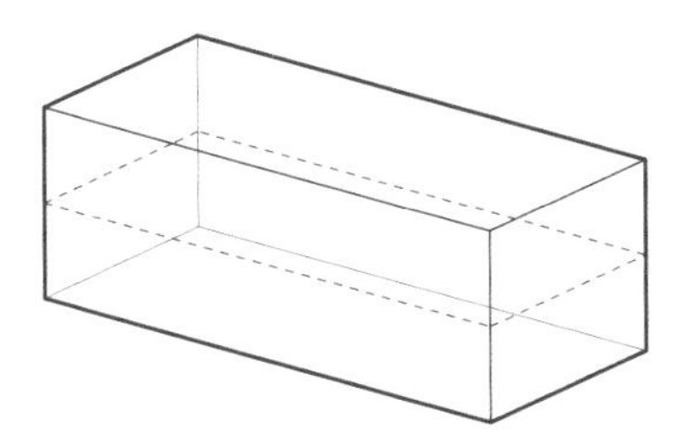

REMOVE SECOND FLOOR AND ADD BREAKOUT LEARNING SPACES

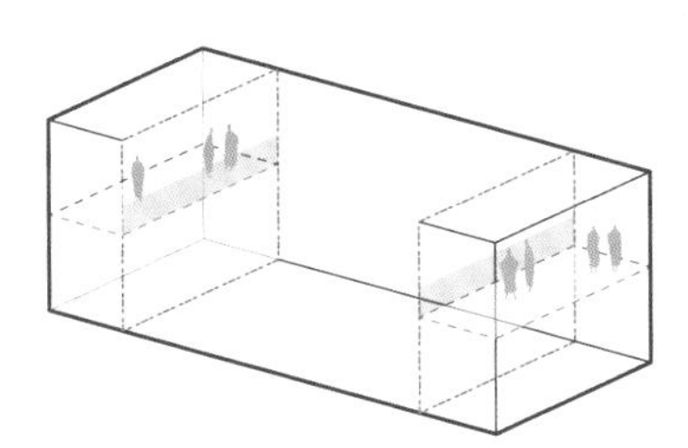

ACTIVATE SURFACE IN COMMUNAL GATHERING SPACE

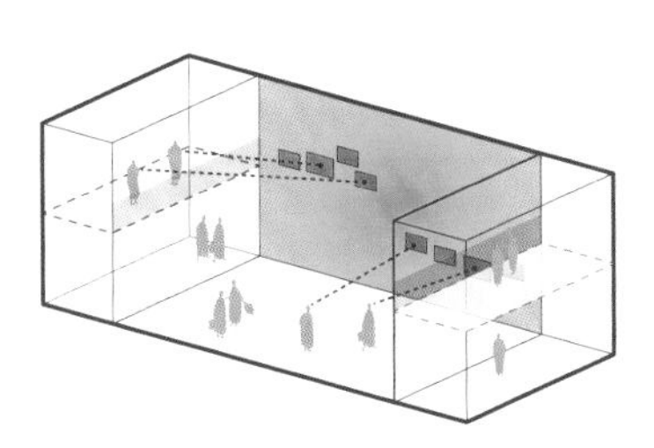

RESHAPE SURFACE

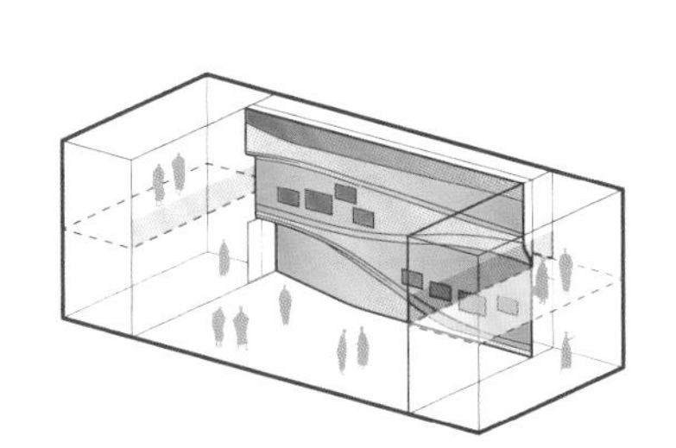

ABOVE: The lobby was reconceived as a double-height space with multiple vantage points for engaging the Global Forum media wall (OPPOSITE), which comprises a series of double-layer glass panels with a printed PVB interlayer formed by CNC-milled foam molds (BELOW LEFT). The interlayer was tested for color and transparency (BELOW MIDDLE) before being attached to a structural steel frame (BELOW RIGHT).

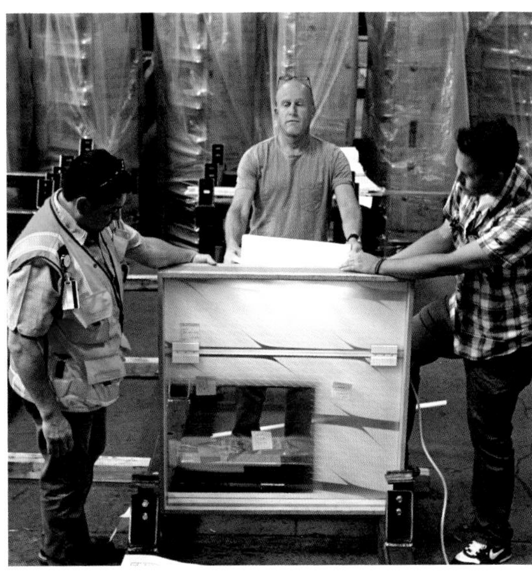

AUDITORIUM

EXISTING

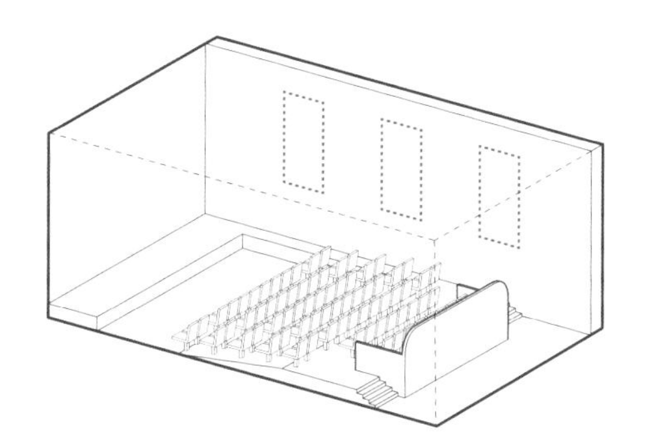

NEW

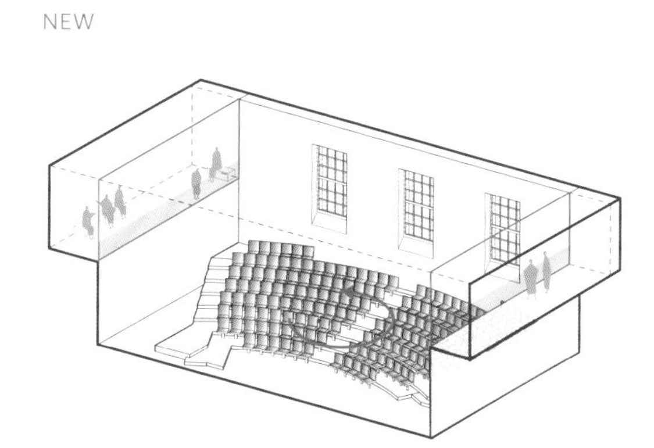

ABOVE: The original orientation of the auditorium was rotated 90 degrees to create a wider, shallower, and more intimate space for instructors and students.

OPPOSITE: Windows were added looking into the small classrooms flanking the auditorium on the third floor to increase capacity and allow these rooms access to ongoing lectures and presentations.

ABOVE: Upgraded lighting is used to define thresholds in the circulation spaces.

OPPOSITE: The media wall's colored LED lighting can coordinate with various forms of graphic presentations.

7

PREVIOUS PAGES: The play of transparency and opacity in the glass curtain wall facade of the Gores Group Headquarters changes throughout the day.

ABOVE: The building is a landmark at the entrance to Beverly Hills, adding drama and significance of place with its highly textured and reflective facade.

Gores Group Headquarters

BEVERLY HILLS, CALIFORNIA, U.S.A.
2010–2014

The Gores Group Headquarters is located at the western gateway of Beverly Hills. The holistic approach to renovating this existing three-story building and the adjacent parking structure focused equally on creating a unique identity for the Gores Group at this prominent site and providing a healthy, enjoyable place for employees and visitors.

First and foremost, the redesign responds to the client's desire to improve office culture. Carving out a new atrium at the center of the main office building and adding an elegant, generous staircase encouraged staff to use more active circulation spaces, increasing impromptu conversations and interaction. This move has also drastically increased the natural lighting and ventilation reaching each floor, and together with the addition of a large communal rooftop terrace and garden, the design has helped improve the health and happiness of employees, and the connectivity and camaraderie among them.

The transformation of the two structures, now connected by an interior bridge across a public thoroughfare, includes several bespoke features and material investigations. Most visible among them is the development of a new modular, slumped-glass panel system used on the facade. The customized pattern within each glass panel selectively filters views and provides privacy and light based on site conditions and the user's needs. Although there are only eight unique patterns, the panels are configured such that the overall design does not repeat itself across the facade. In addition, the appearance of the slumped glass changes depending on natural lighting conditions, creating a truly dynamic entrance or exit to the city.

WILSHIRE BLVD.

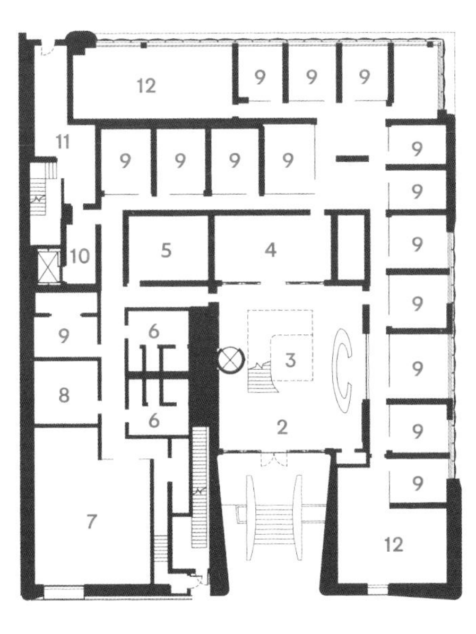

1

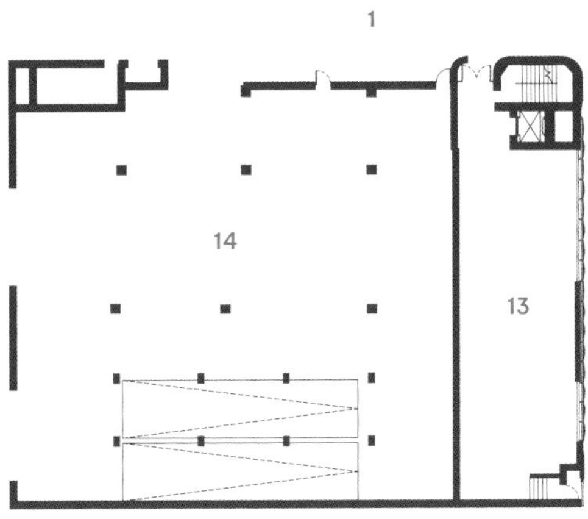

SOUTH SPAULDING DRIVE

GROUND FLOOR PLAN
1 PRIVATE MOTOR ENTRANCE
2 LOBBY
3 ATRIUM
4 CONFERENCE ROOM
5 COPY ROOM
6 RESTROOM
7 EMPLOYEE LOUNGE
8 STAFF PANTRY/KITCHEN
9 OFFICE
10 ELEVATOR LOBBY
11 PRIVATE ENTRANCE
12 OPEN OFFICE AREA
13 FITNESS CENTER
14 PARKING

FACADE DEVELOPMENT

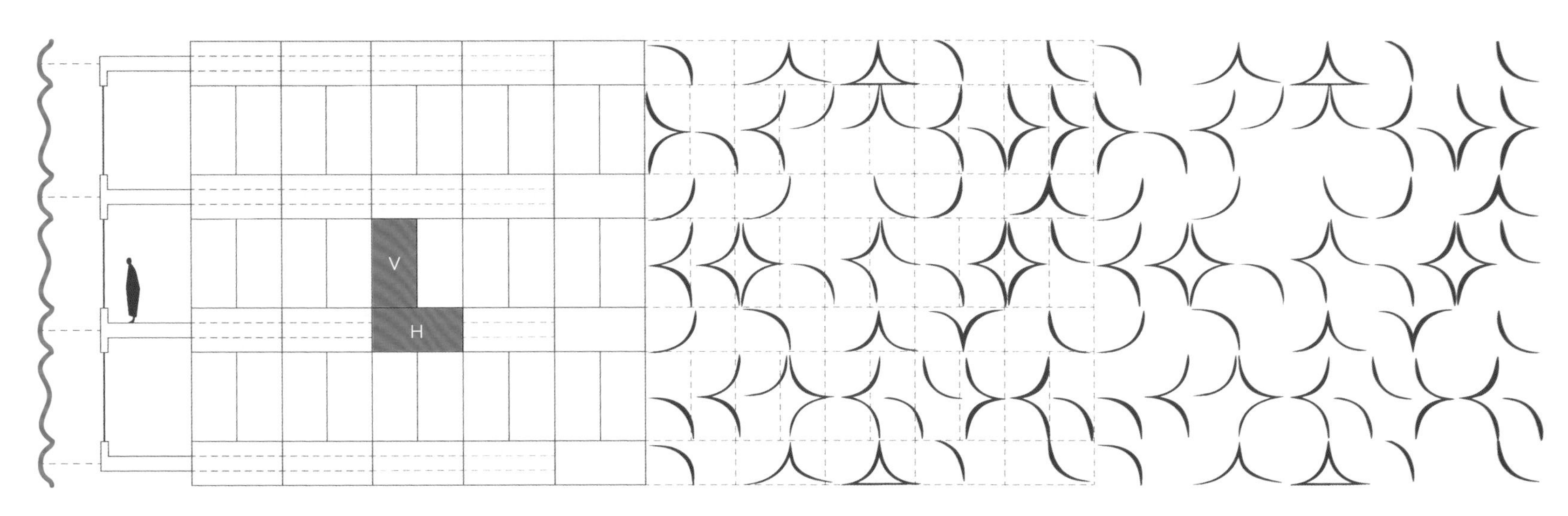

ABOVE: A unitized system of glass panels is overlaid with a pattern of curves that, when aggregated, diffuse the familiar reading of alternating floor slabs and vision glass. The pillowy form and reflective material quality of the panels further enhance this effect.

SLUMPED GLASS

PRINTED PVB INTERLAYER

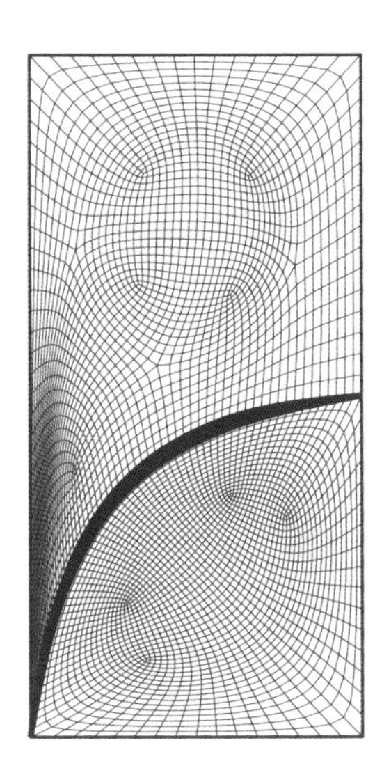

OPPOSITE AND LEFT: Each panel is embedded with a layering of material qualities including transparency, reflectivity, curvature, and graphics.

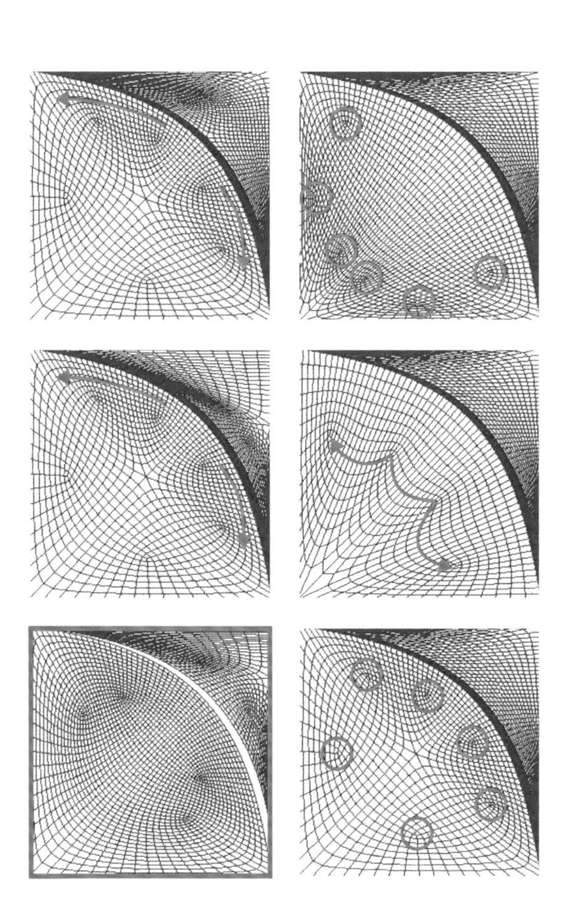

RIGHT: The geometry of the glass panels was carefully developed to increase strength and resistance to seismic and wind loads while also informing the final printed frit pattern.

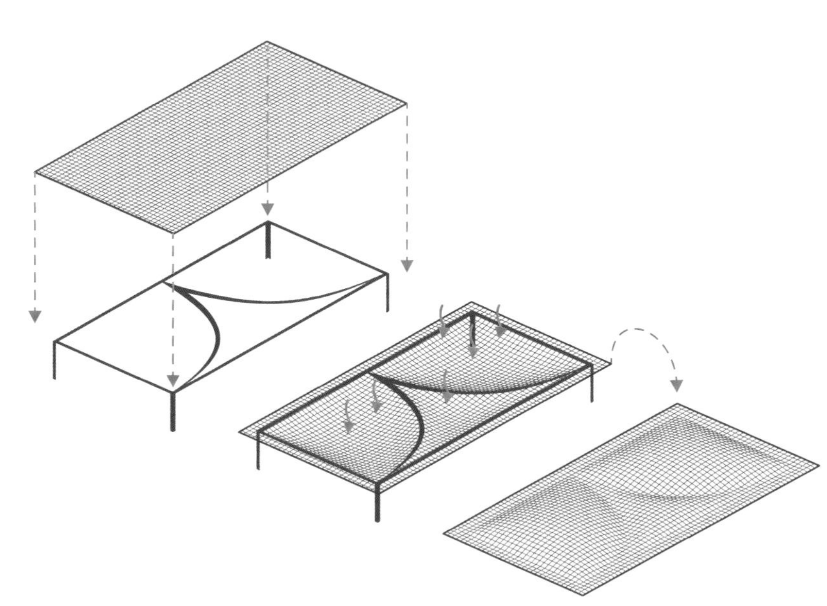

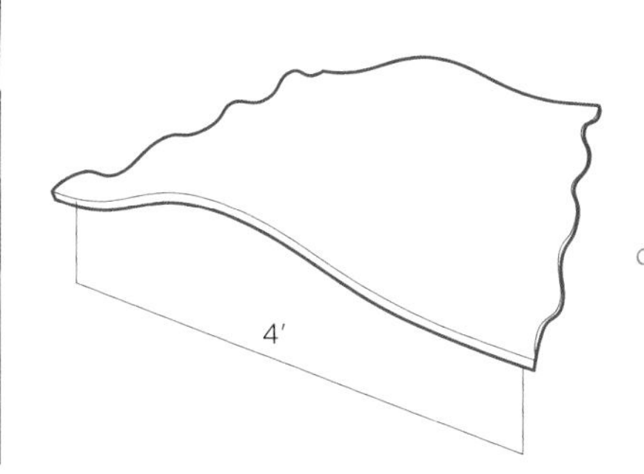

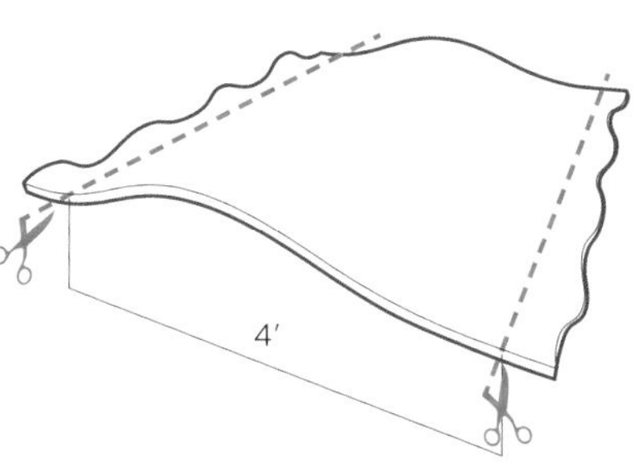

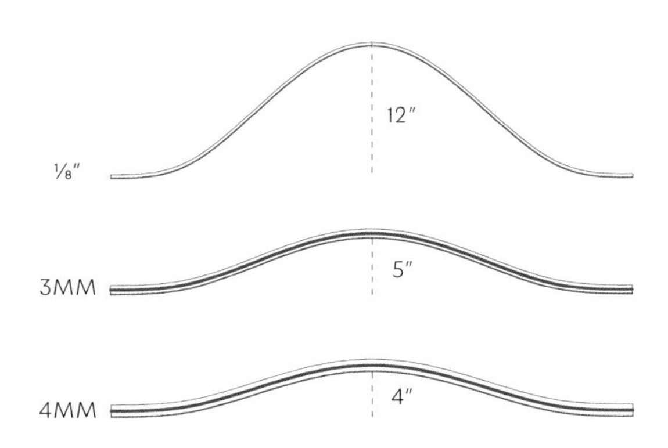

Variation in the deformation of the laminated panels was limited by the glass's structural integrity, durability of the system, and pattern alignment of the PVB layer.

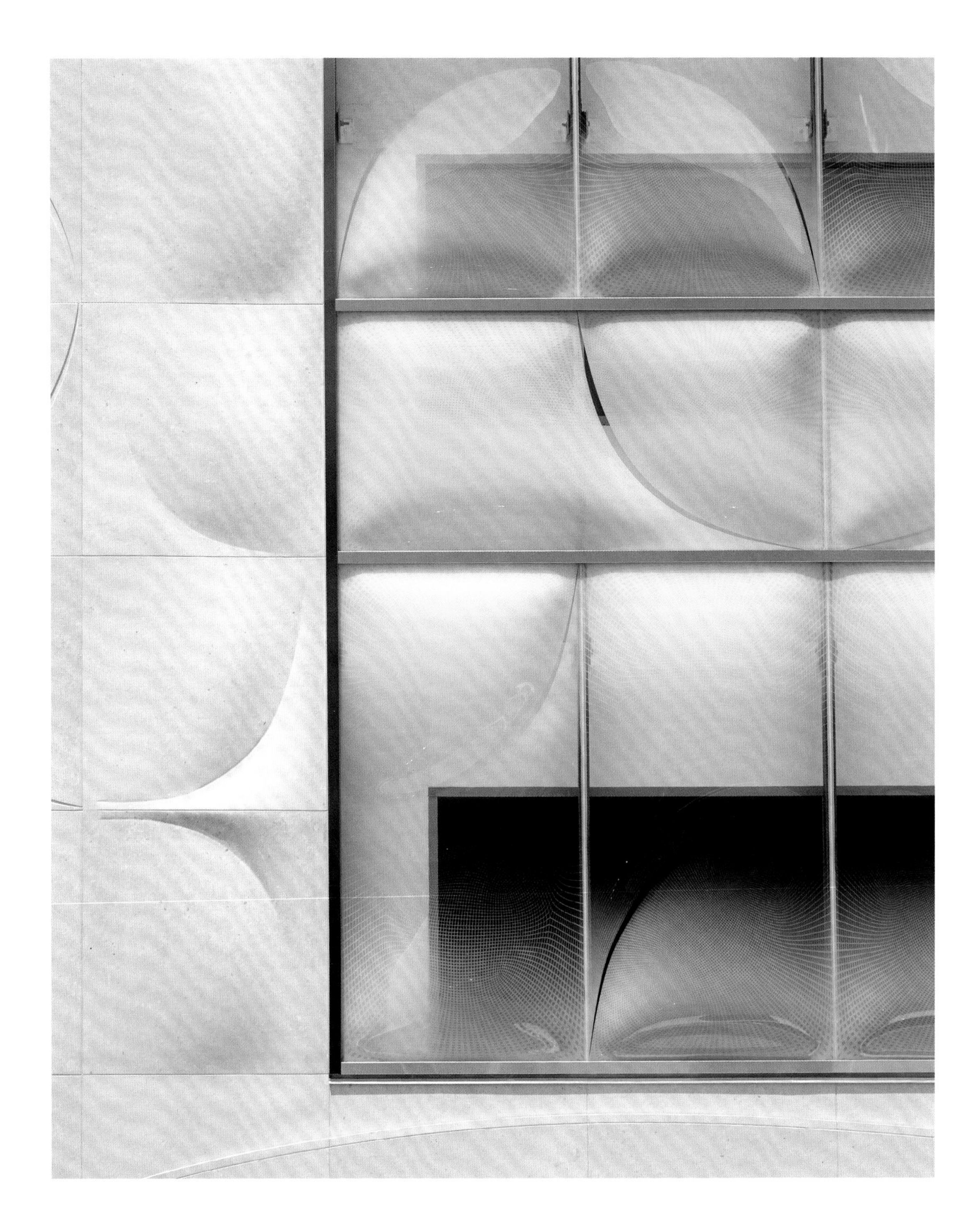

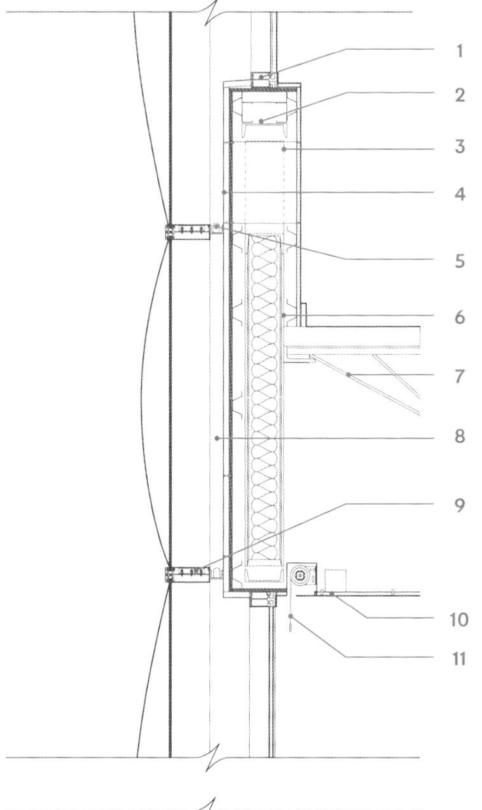

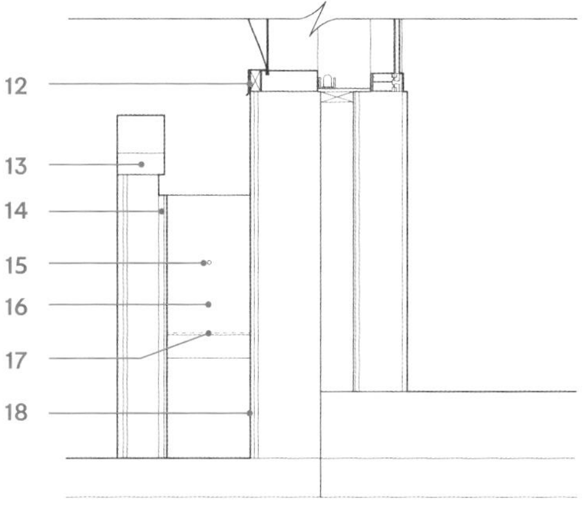

FACADE SECTION DETAIL

1 INTERIOR FIXED STOREFRONT SYSTEM
2 EXISTING TRUSS WITH FIRE PROOFING
3 INTERIOR FURRING STUD WALL
4 LIGHT FIXTURE ACCESS PANELS
5 LED LIGHTING
6 EXISTING OPEN WEB TRUSS JOISTS
7 EXISTING SLAB EDGE ON STEEL ANGLE
8 EXTERIOR STUD WALL, WITH ½″ DENSSHIELD SUBSTRATE WATERPROOFING MEMBRANE STUCCO FINISH
9 2 ¼″ X 7″ T-500 ARCADIA CURTAIN WALL SYSTEM
10 LIGHT FIXTURE ACCESS PANELS EVERY 16′ APPROX.
11 ROLLER SHADE FLUSH WITH DROPPED CEILING SYSTEM
12 STAINLESS STEEL CAP TO MATCH CURTAIN WALL SYSTEM
13 UNDULATING PLANTER WALL CLAD WITH 2″ STONE CAP
14 SELF-ADHERED, RUBBERIZED ASPHALT WATERPROOFING MEMBRANE
15 DRIP IRRIGATION SYSTEM
16 LIGHTWEIGHT GROWING MEDIUM
17 HYDRODUCT GEOCOMPOSITE DRAINAGE
18 PONY WALL SUPPORTING CURTAIN WALL CLAD WITH STONE

The field of the slumped-glass curtain wall panels gives way to the double envelope system upon approach.

ABOVE: A new formal entrance was carved out of the rear elevation, replacing the existing utility alley with a luxury valet lobby.

OPPOSITE AND FOLLOWING PAGES: Custom wood guardrails incorporate built-in lighting to create a sweeping fluidity throughout the stair.

OPPOSITE: A skylight washes natural light into the sculptural stair.

ABOVE: A screened trellis shades the garden roof-deck and a recessed courtyard beyond allows for greater penetration of daylight into the offices.

FOLLOWING PAGES: An interior bridge elegantly links the parking structure to the office building.

PARK
120 S. SPALDING
PARKING
LeFrak Organization

8

PREVIOUS PAGES: A floating concrete bench on the campus of the Pavilion at City of Hope provides seating beneath the shade of a camphor tree.

ABOVE: The West Building's undulating concrete wall is embedded with an array of lights.

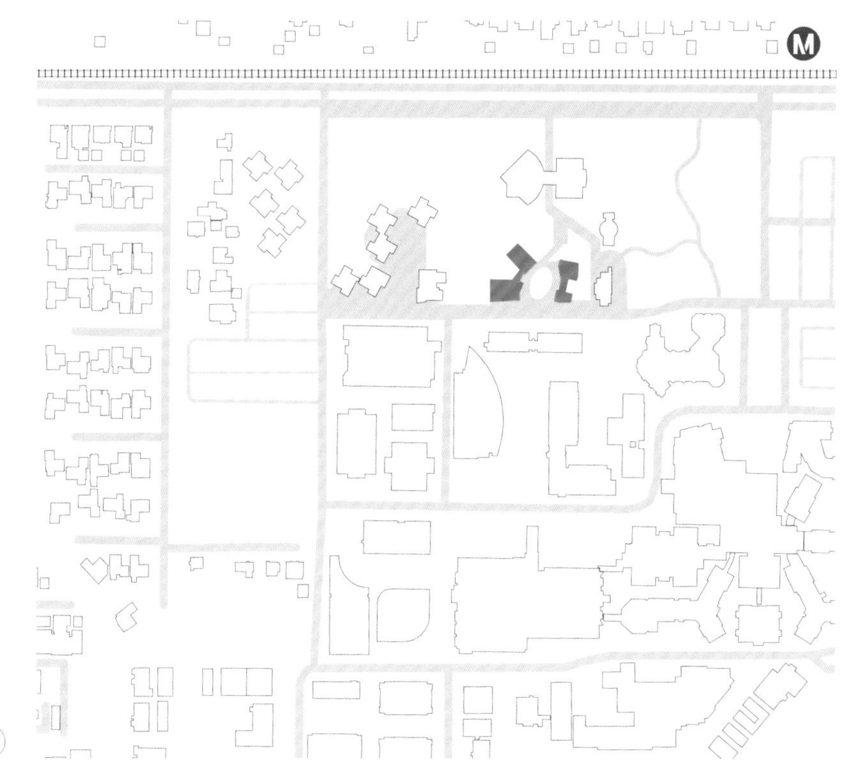

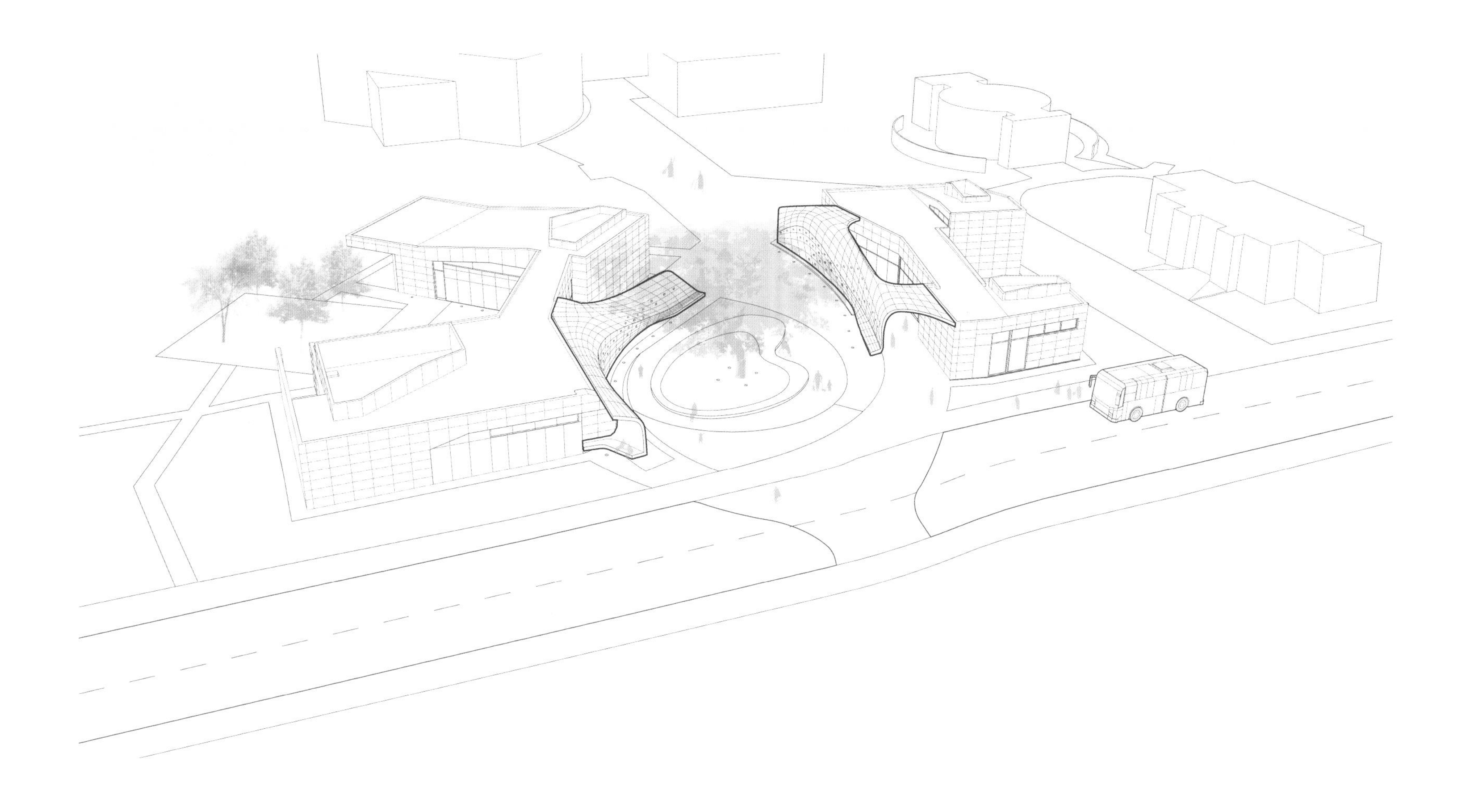

The Pavilion at City of Hope

DUARTE, CALIFORNIA, U.S.A.
2010–2015

City of Hope, a leading research and treatment center for cancer, diabetes, and other life-threatening diseases, marked its centennial with the addition of a new, multifaceted space at the heart of its Duarte, California, campus. The LEED Platinum project comprises 7,000 square feet across two buildings (the West Building and the East Building) used to host lectures, exhibitions, events, and administrative offices. The structures open to the north, reducing excessive heat gain and exposure and providing a visual connection between the occupants and the surrounding landscape.

Inspired by wishing trees, the Pavilion at City of Hope's siting realigns an off-axis promenade on the campus grid and wraps around a camphor tree that was planted near the time City of Hope was founded. The two single-story structures encircle the tree, forming curved, concrete walls that twist into a contemplative seating area; protected sight lines provide additional privacy and sound buffering to those enjoying this outdoor sanctuary. Along the surface of the walls, LED-lit niches highlight City of Hope's many milestones, while leaving room for future accomplishments to be noted. The prominence of the tree in relation to the buildings draws a strong connection between the institution's heritage and its site, and creates a new amenity for anyone on campus.

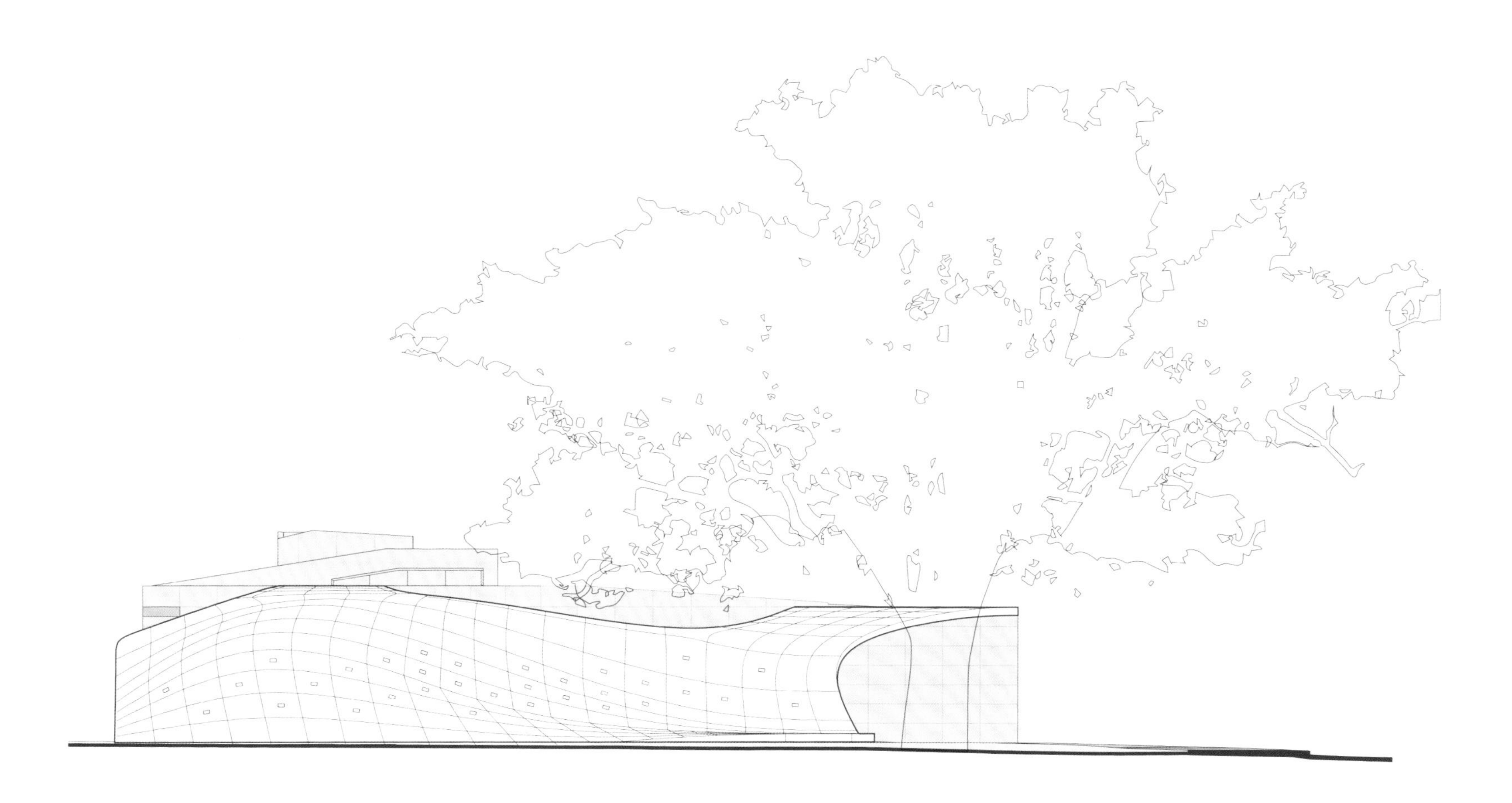

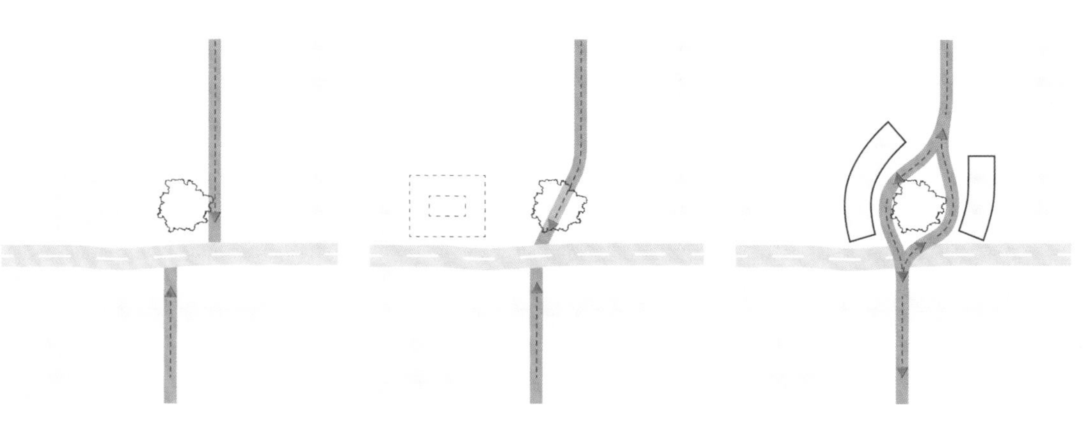

OPPOSITE AND ABOVE: The architecture's undulating concrete facades and integrated benches maneuver around an existing camphor tree.

RIGHT: Campus circulation was rerouted to divert traffic around the tree.

LEFT: Plywood formwork and rebar were used to create the facades of the two buildings so they could envelop the main courtyard space and the camphor tree (ABOVE AND OPPOSITE).

FOLLOWING PAGES: The East Building's concrete wall hovers above the ground to form a bench.

ARTHUR & ROSALIE KAPLAN FAMILY PAVILION
City of Hope

OPPOSITE AND ABOVE: The main assembly space extends into the City of Hope campus.

FOLLOWING PAGES: The sensitive integration of formed materials and nature evokes tranquility throughout the day.

9

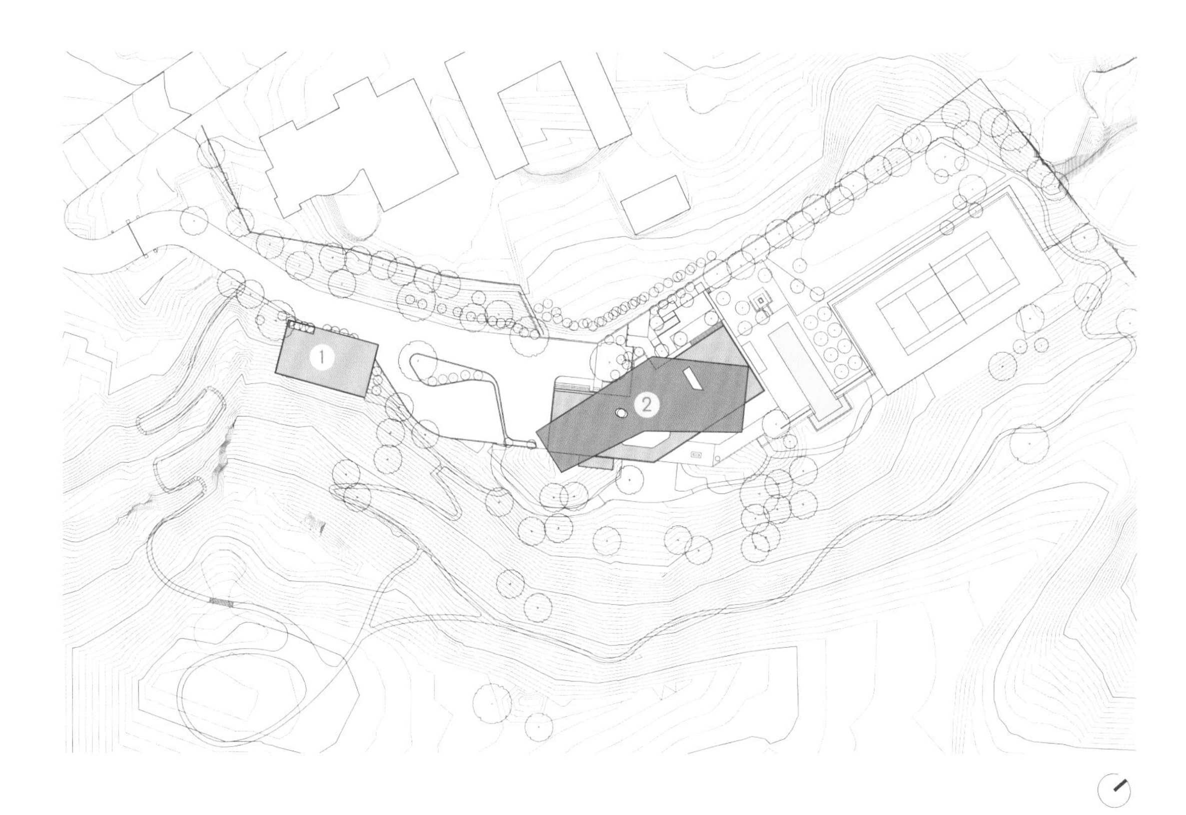

SITE PLAN
1 GUESTHOUSE
2 MAIN HOUSE

Tree Top Residence

LOS ANGELES, CALIFORNIA, U.S.A.
2010–2015

The Tree Top Residence strikes a balance between responding to its complex site and providing privacy for its occupants. Hidden from the street, the house is insulated from its neighbors, but open to its site. Canted limestone louvers, and dense planting on the west facade shield the interior from the closest neighbor. Conversely, the rest of the building opens to the site with floor-to-ceiling glazing, relying on both the house's generous distance from the property line, and the densely wooded valley below to create a natural screen.

The three-story house follows the natural ridgeline of the sloping landscape. The building's long and narrow plan mimics and inverts the angles of the site's topography, creating dynamic horizontal and vertical relationships. Horizontally, walls are used sparingly in favor of open and connected spaces. Movement and views between dining areas, the kitchen, and play and gathering spaces are uninterrupted, and pocket sliding glass doors blur the line between inside and out. Vertically, an eccentrically helical stair functions as a primary organizing element and a sculptural gesture upon entry. On the ground floor, it acts as a threshold of the open plan; on the floor above, it separates the main suite and children's quarter; and finally, it provides a light well to the basement. The residence emerges atop the canopy of trees that surround it; the orchestration of the view embodies the intent to offer respite from the city below.

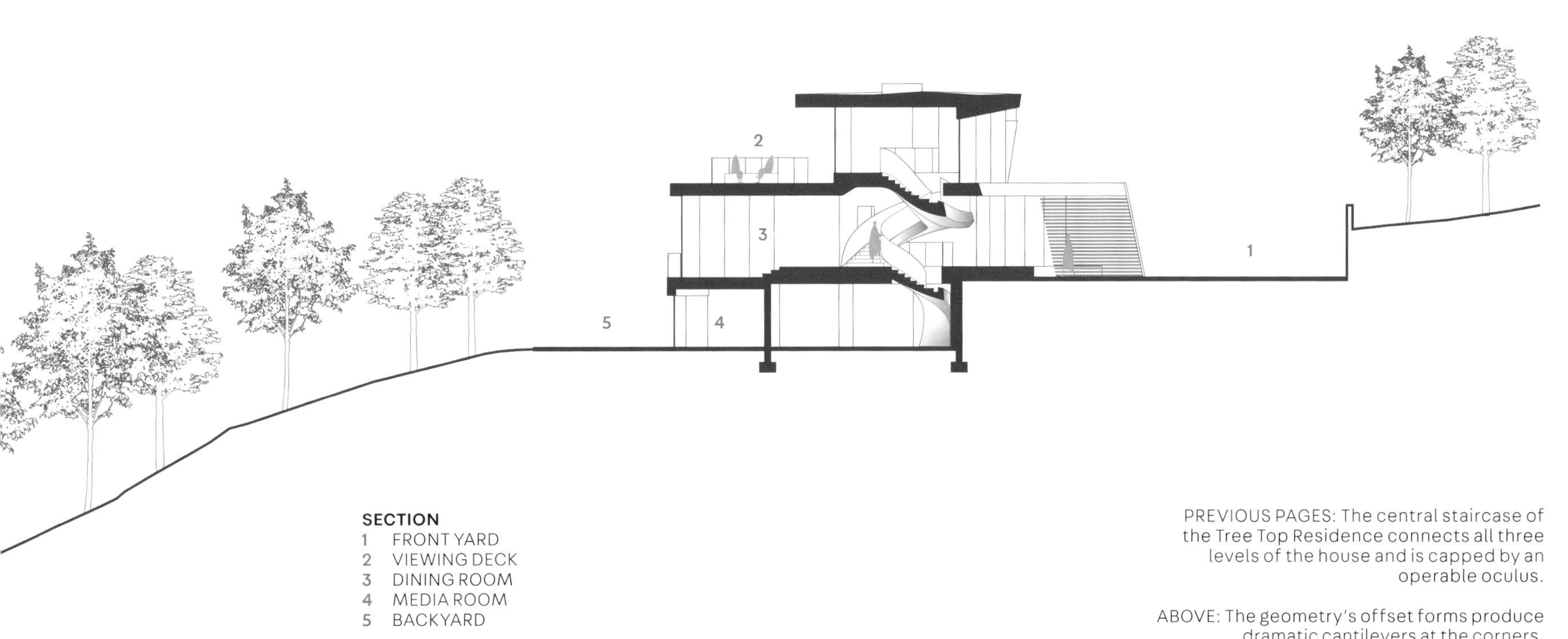

SECTION
1 FRONT YARD
2 VIEWING DECK
3 DINING ROOM
4 MEDIA ROOM
5 BACKYARD

PREVIOUS PAGES: The central staircase of the Tree Top Residence connects all three levels of the house and is capped by an operable oculus.

ABOVE: The geometry's offset forms produce dramatic cantilevers at the corners.

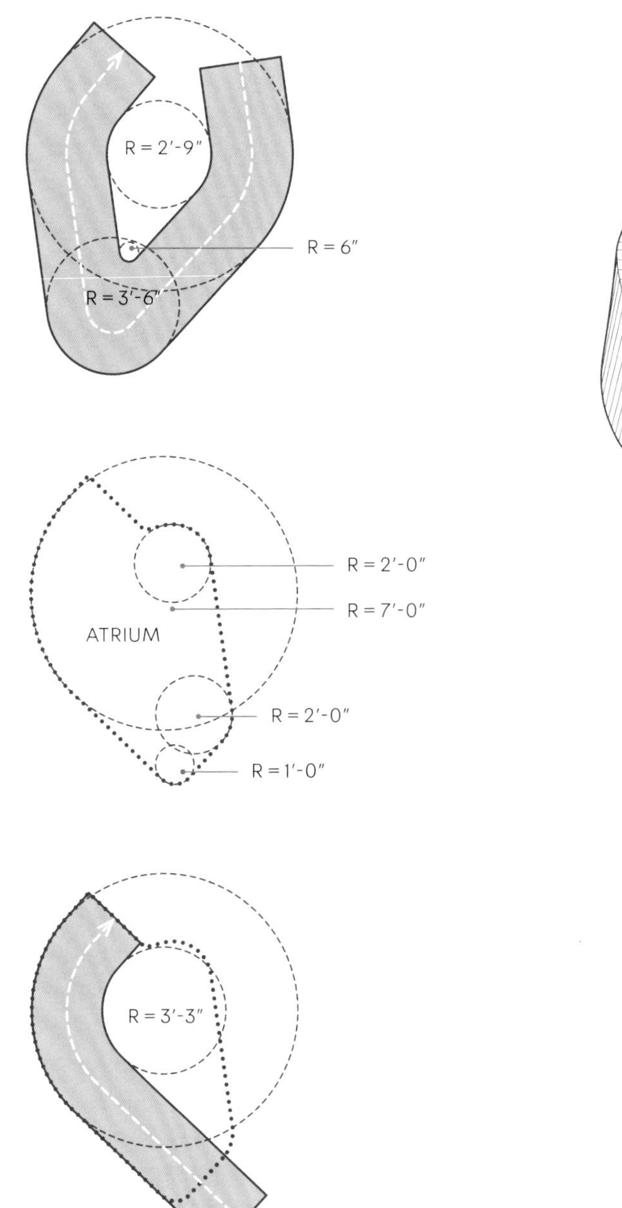

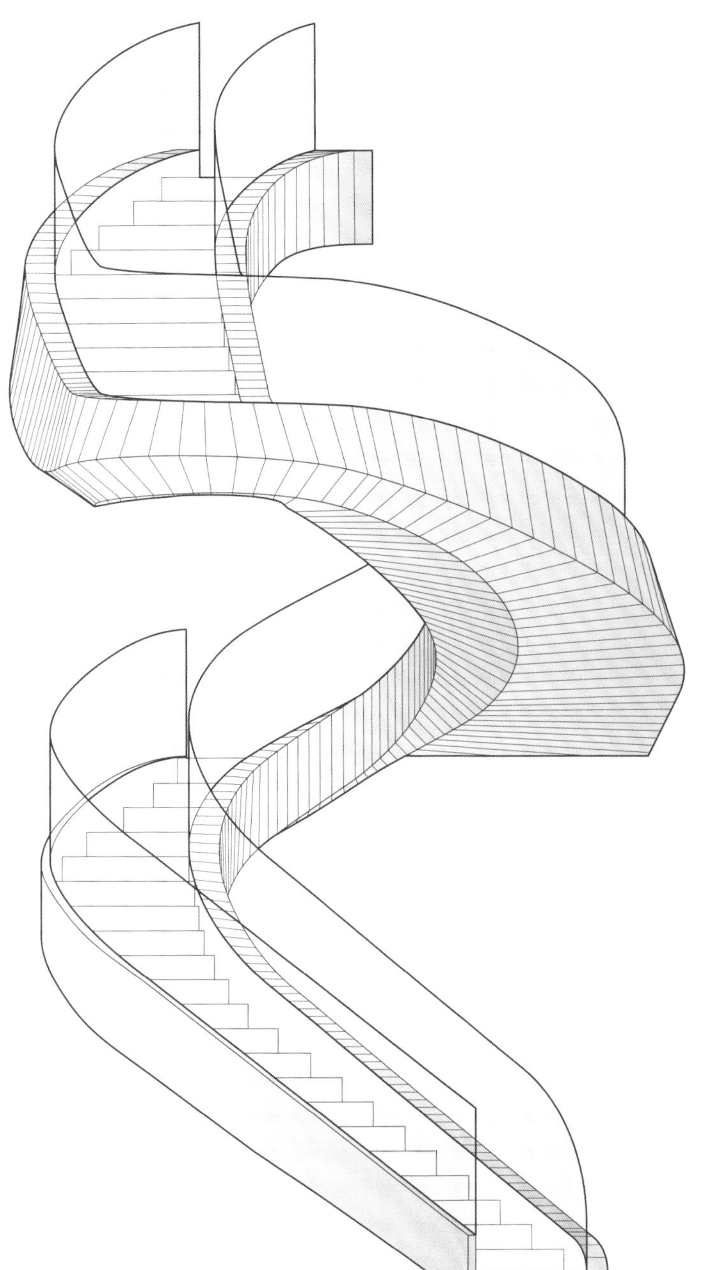

The stair's geometry is a product of the difference between the basement, ground floor, and second floor volumes and minimum code requirements for the radii of a stair. Hung from the second floor, the stair offers a continuous void from the second floor down to the basement. It has no visible vertical structure, allowing for light to pass through.

The stair was assembled from 1-inch-thick bent steel stringers and ⅜-inch-thick steel treads and risers fabricated in a workshop in three sections and craned into place (LEFT). This structure was clad in plywood ribs to create the profile of the stringer cladding, then sheathed with bending lauan plywood, and finished with strips of individually placed European white oak (BELOW AND OPPOSITE).

FOLLOWING PAGES: From the top floor, a view of the basement, three floors below, features a small seating area.

STAIR CONSTRUCTION DETAIL

1 STEEL STRINGER
2 STEEL STAIR
3 WOOD JIG
4 BENDING LAUAN PLYWOOD SUBSTRATE
5 CURVED GLASS PANELS
6 WHITE EUROPEAN OAK STRIPS
7 SPINE

OPPOSITE: Guests that arrive at the front door pass first beneath a stone-louvered screen.

ABOVE: A push and pull between interior and exterior is evident with floor-to-ceiling sliding glass doors that open the kitchen and dining areas to the outside gathering spaces.

FOLLOWING PAGES: From the rear yard, the massing of the opposing and stacked forms is more clearly viewed.

10

PREVIOUS PAGES AND ABOVE: The double curvature and structural integrity of the facade elements required considerable research and development of materials, shapes, and fabrication methods.

FOURTH FLOOR

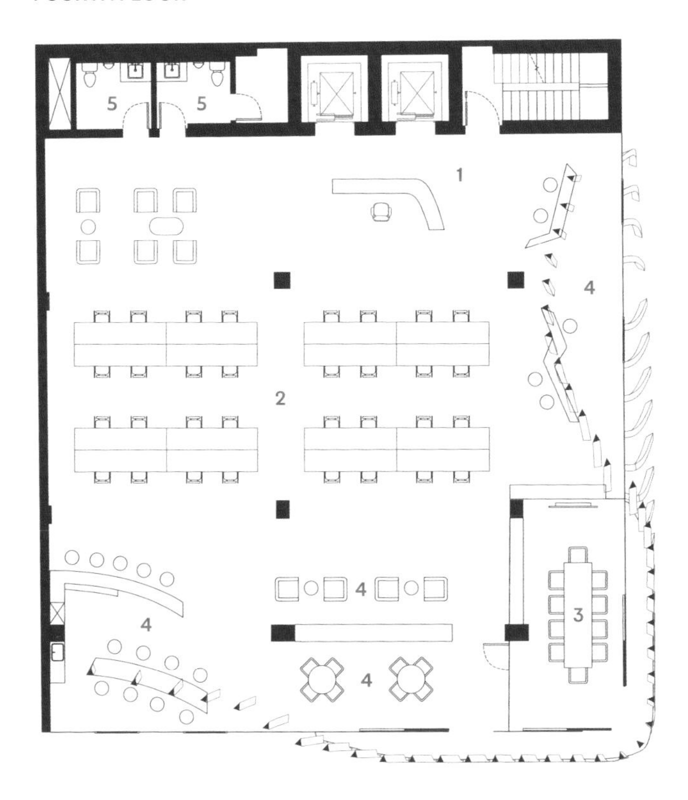

SIXTH FLOOR

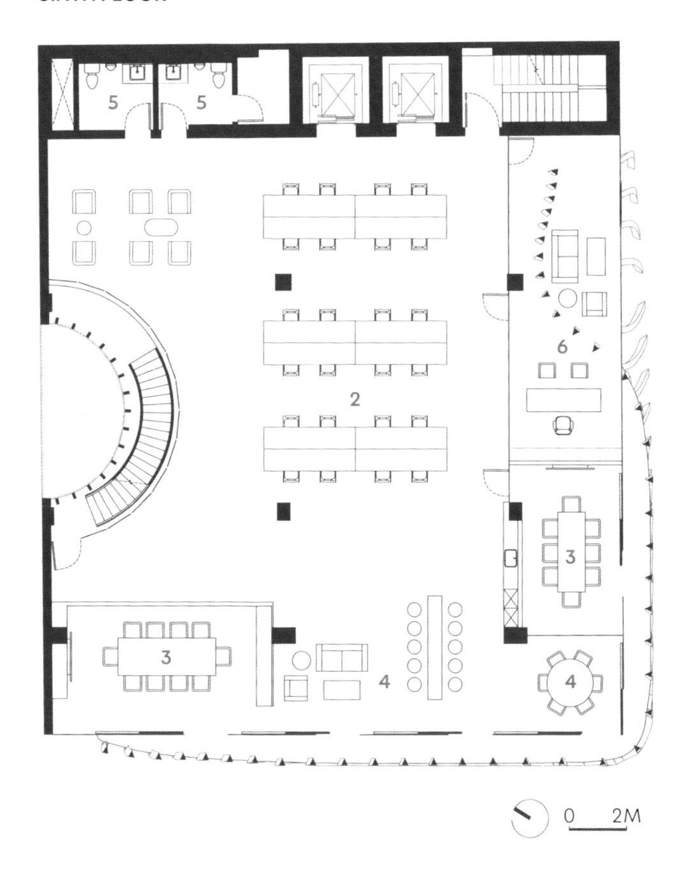

FLOOR PLANS
1 RECEPTION
2 WORK STATIONS
3 CONFERENCE ROOM
4 BREAKOUT SPACE
5 RESTROOM
6 PRIVATE OFFICE

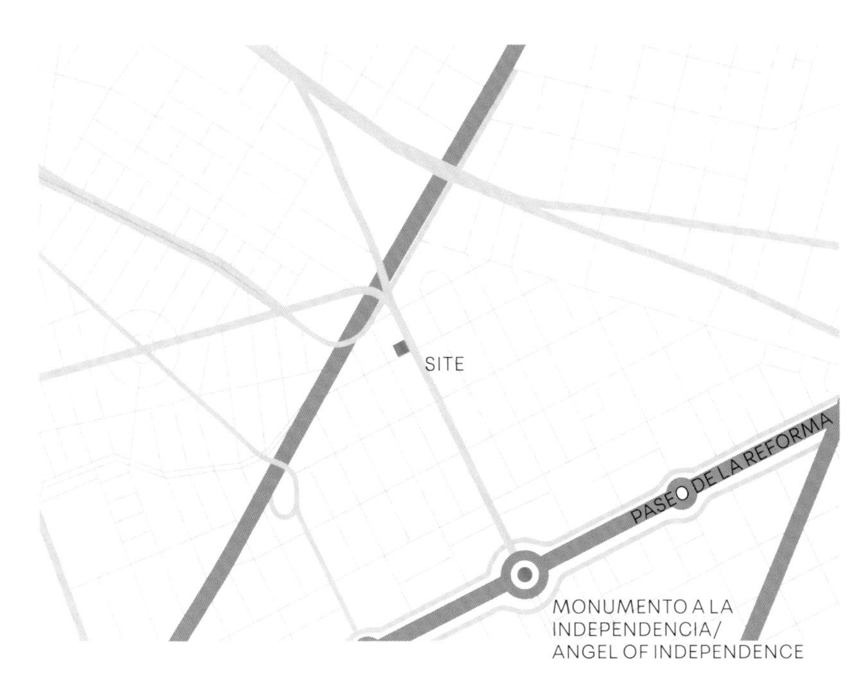

Threads

MEXICO CITY, MEXICO
2013–2016

Facades are often thought of as an exterior skin. However, Threads, a low-rise office building in Mexico City, features a fluid, habitable facade that moves in and out of the building. A series of sinuous vertical elements that appear to penetrate the six-story curtain wall, these "fins" dissolve the solidity of the building envelope, shape interior and exterior niches, and add depth and movement to the facade's fixed plane.

With the Mexican headquarters of the French premium wine and spirits company Pernod Ricard, the prominent corner siting of this six-story building prompted us to explore the function and form of its two street-facing elevations. By pushing the elevator, stairs, and restrooms to one edge of the building, we freed the plan to provide flexibility in layout and maximize unobstructed views to the street and city beyond. Digital design tools and digital fabrication techniques were used to create 272 unique, three-dimensionally curving aluminum fins that attach to the glazing and concrete slabs. Their triangular geometry allows, among other things, for the welded forms to achieve the desired curvature without additional jigs or molds. These elements, each spanning one story, required precision during installation to achieve alignment and visual continuity. Their arrangement, which varies from floor to floor, creates unique spatial opportunities on each level. Gray, laminated glazing with a low-emissivity coating was also employed to reduce heat gain and affects the visibility of the interior over the course of the day, further elevating the dynamism of the building's presence to users and people on the street below.

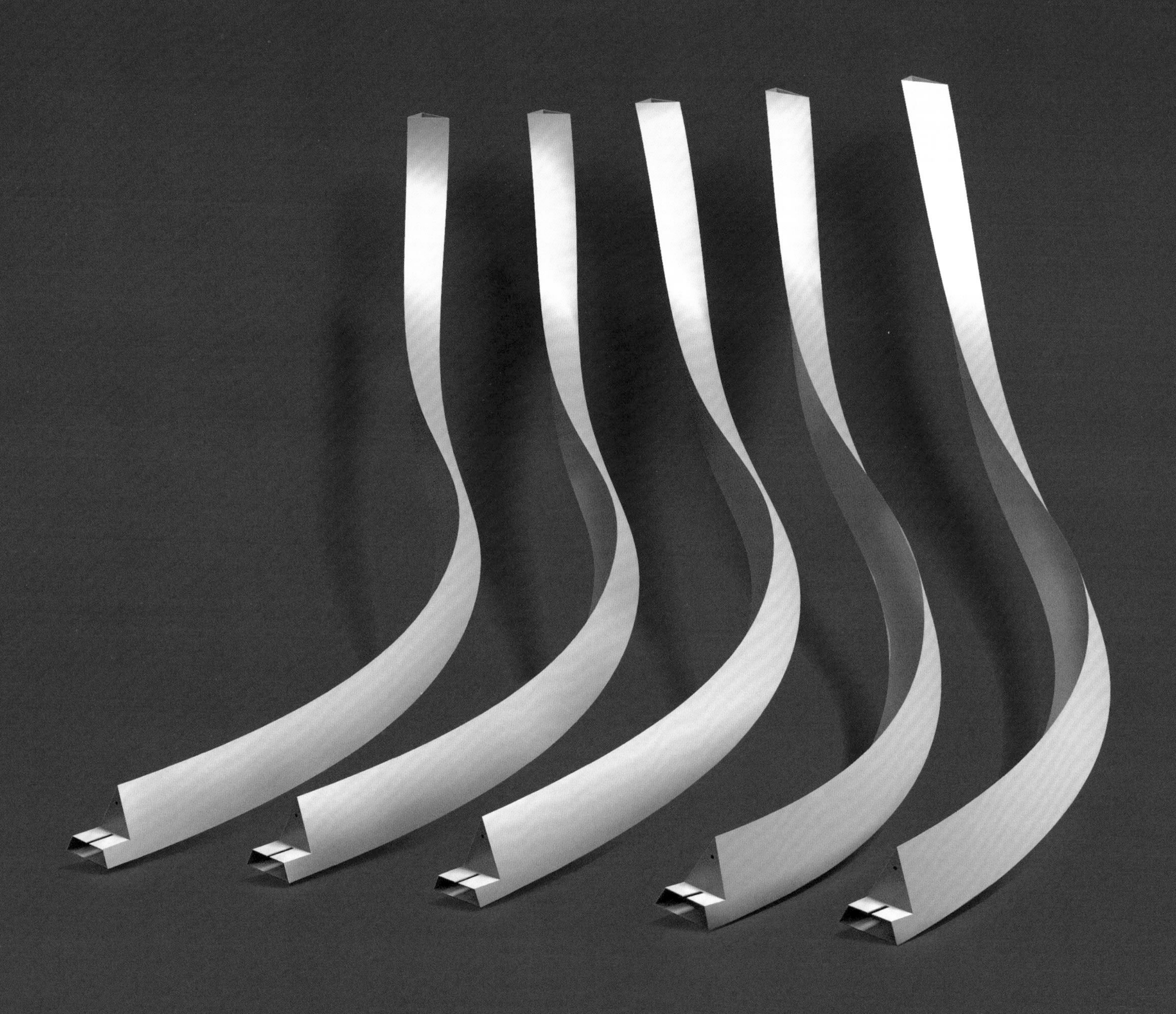

DIAGRAMMATIC SECTION

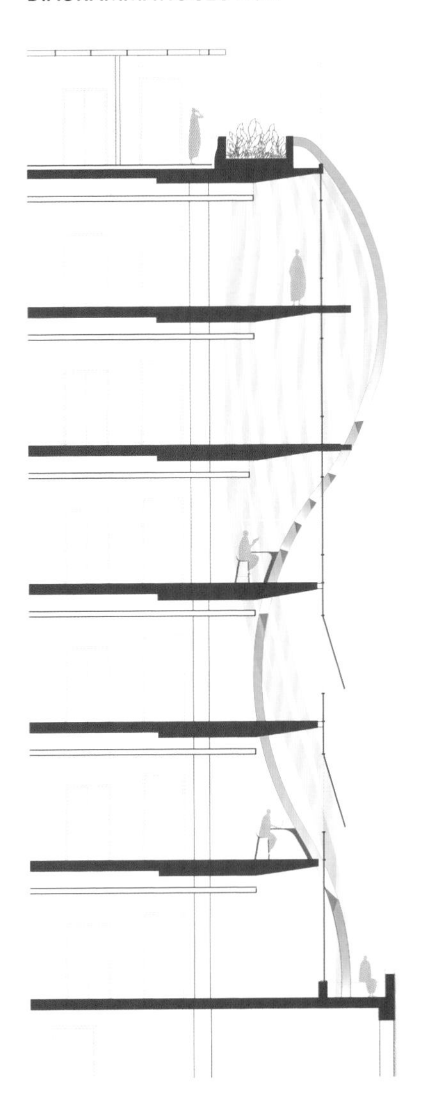

UNROLLED FIN ELEMENTS

ASSEMBLED FIN

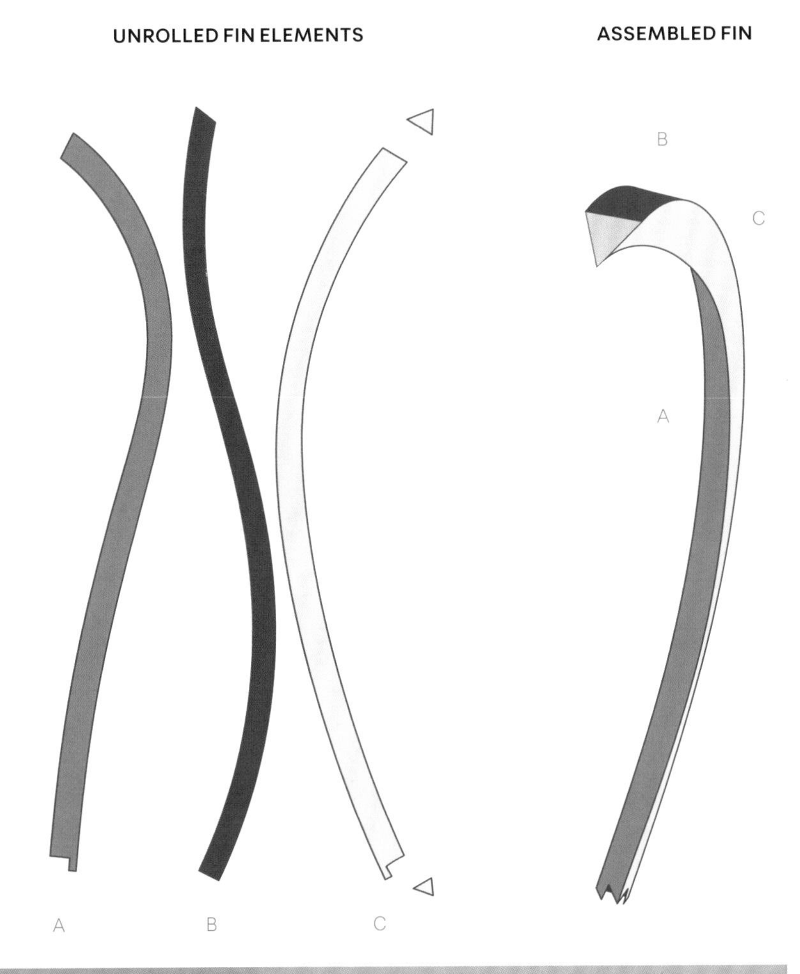

Threads's rooftop terrace offers a skyline bar and event venue.

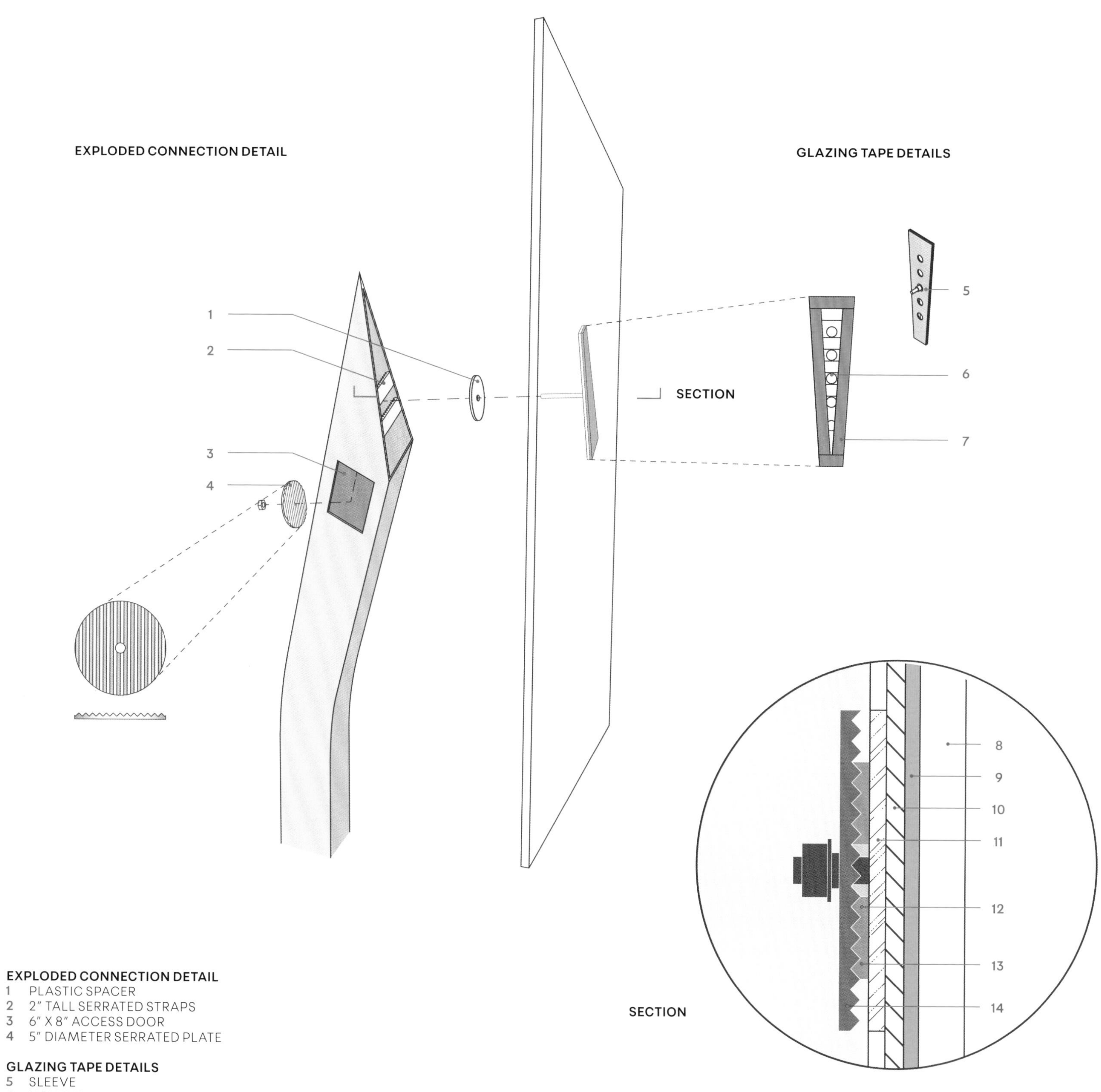

EXPLODED CONNECTION DETAIL
1 PLASTIC SPACER
2 2" TALL SERRATED STRAPS
3 6" X 8" ACCESS DOOR
4 5" DIAMETER SERRATED PLATE

GLAZING TAPE DETAILS
5 SLEEVE
6 HOLES THAT ALLOW PLACEMENT OF STUD TO BE ADJUSTED
7 3M VHB STRUCTURAL GLAZING TAPE

SECTION (GLASS CONNECTION)
8 LAMINATED GLASS
9 3M VHB GLAZING TAPE
10 STAINLESS STEEL PLATE WITH THREADED STUD
11 PLASTIC SPACER
12 NYLON LOCKNUT
13 2" TALL SERRATED STRAPS
14 5" DIAMETER SERRATED PLATE

The indoor-outdoor transition of the facade elements is handled by mechanically adhering them to the glass curtain wall with structural glazing tape.

Obscuring and dematerializing the corner of the building while also considering views and sun-shading opportunities—a combination of formal and pragmatic interests—ultimately informed the final placement and movement of the fins.

The fins carve out spatial zones of lounge and collaboration areas as they trace vertically between floor levels.

NUEVO NISSAN
UNA DECISIÓN
VENTA

ABOVE: Various workplace-enhancing activities are possible at the sun-drenched perimeters.

OPPOSITE: The building is illuminated for legibility at night.

CALMEX

The facade, positioned at the nexus of an arterial expressway, emulates the motion and dynamism of the city.

11

The massing of the building is manipulated to invite light and air into the terrace and interstitial spaces.

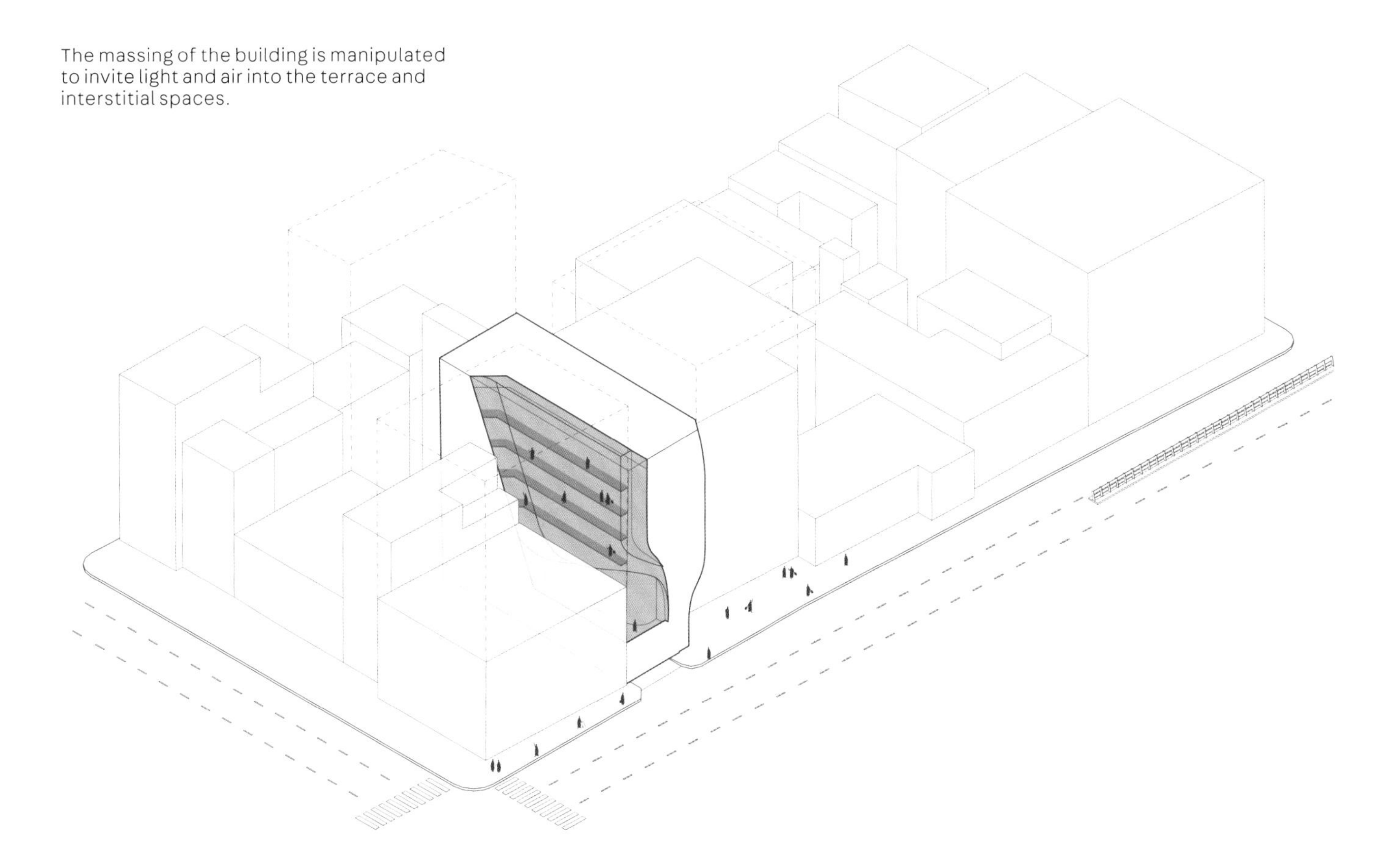

Profiles

MEXICO CITY, MEXICO
2013–2018

Profiles embodies the potential of a mid-block property. The eight-story office building is located on a busy one-way street in the Cuauhtémoc neighborhood of Mexico City and pulls back from its neighbor to the south, maximizing exposure to oncoming vehicular traffic and creating a terrace on the second floor. This addresses a local "open air" building code requirement while giving occupants greater access to daylight and natural ventilation, and increasing the overall visibility of the project.

The two street-facing facades are united by a perforated carbon-steel screen with electrostatic paint that follows the curvature of the building mass. The overall pattern of the perforation emanated from a two-dimensional projection from the point on the street where the two sides are most visible. Using a repeated pattern of enlarging openings, vertical striations emerge, mimicking the tufts of a curtain. Some of the perforated material is left attached to the panels; these chads change in size to add further depth to the facade by softening the appearance of the steel, and at times, dematerializing the panels themselves. The variable angles of the chads also create a dynamic effect as lighting conditions change—at times creating shadows or seeming to disappear completely. Overall, the perforation has been optimized for ventilation and light, and maintains privacy and visibility for occupants. This approach demonstrates new opportunities for mid-block buildings to engage with the street while shaping the user experience.

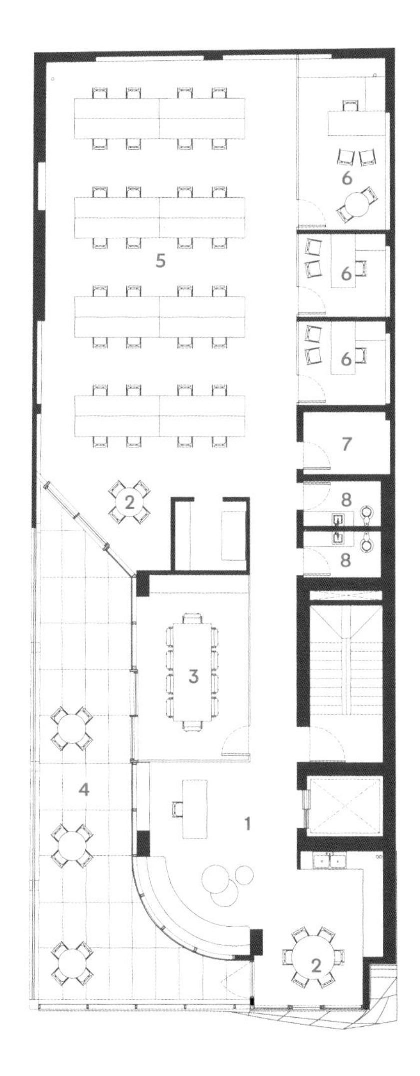

SECOND FLOOR PLAN
1 RECEPTION
2 MEETING AREA
3 CONFERENCE ROOM
4 TERRACE
5 OPEN PLAN OFFICE
6 OFFICE
7 STORAGE
8 RESTROOM

PREVIOUS PAGES: All sides of Profiles contribute visually to the urban experience.

ABOVE: The corner between the street-facing and side facades unseams for light and views.

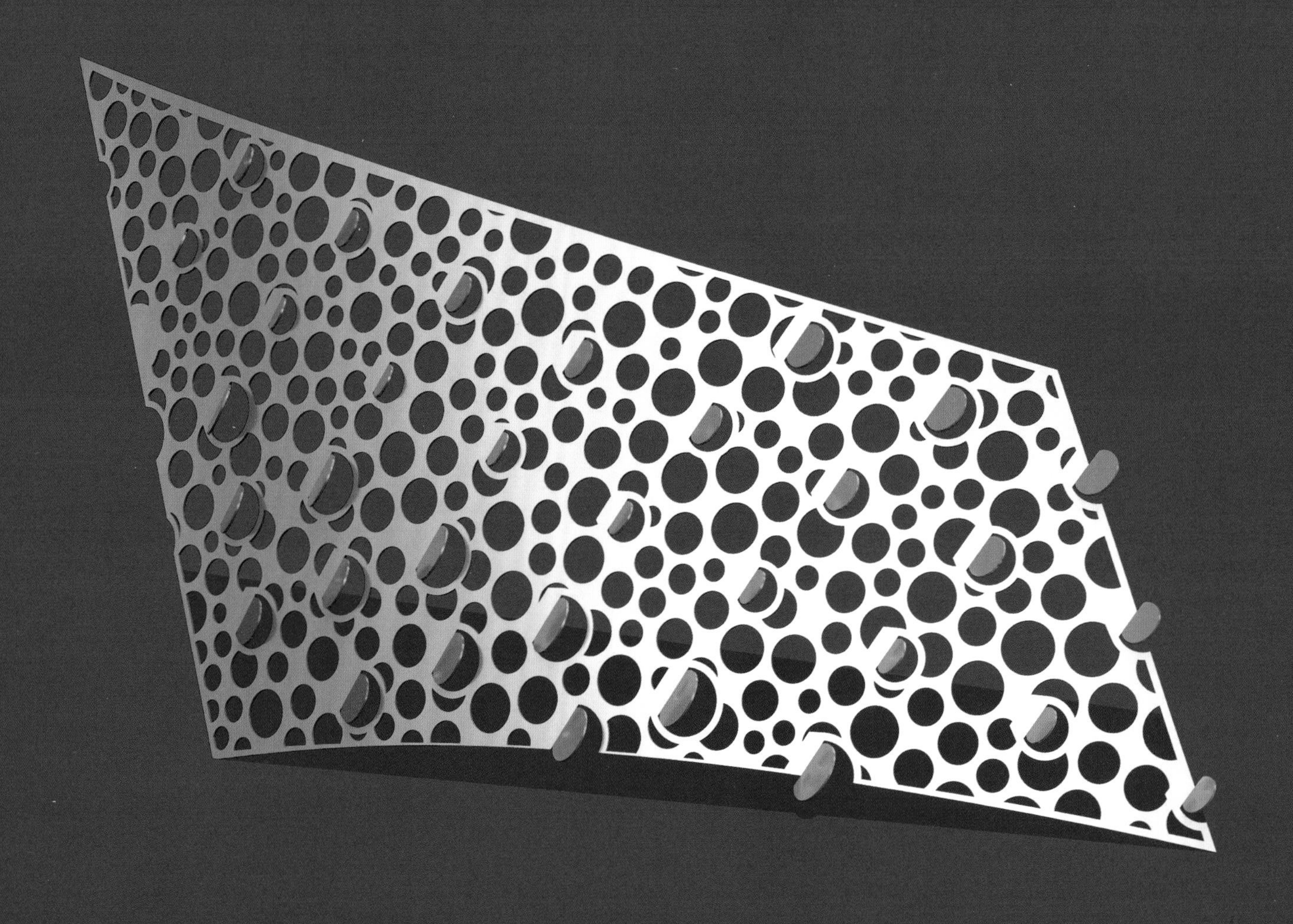

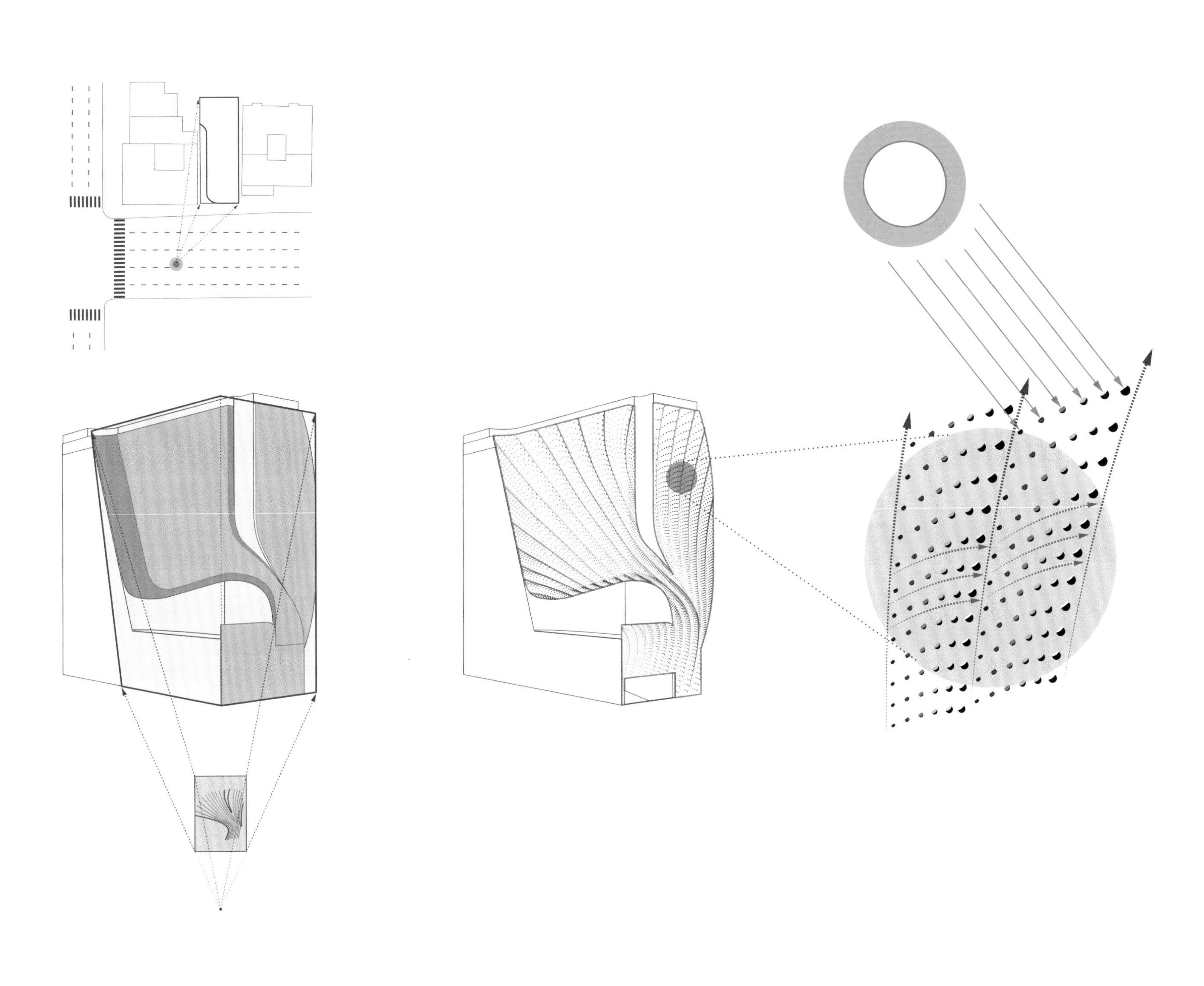

A pattern of folded metal plates is projected onto all facade surfaces from select vantage points on the street. From this corner, the pattern is perceived as two-dimensional regardless of the facade's orientation or form.

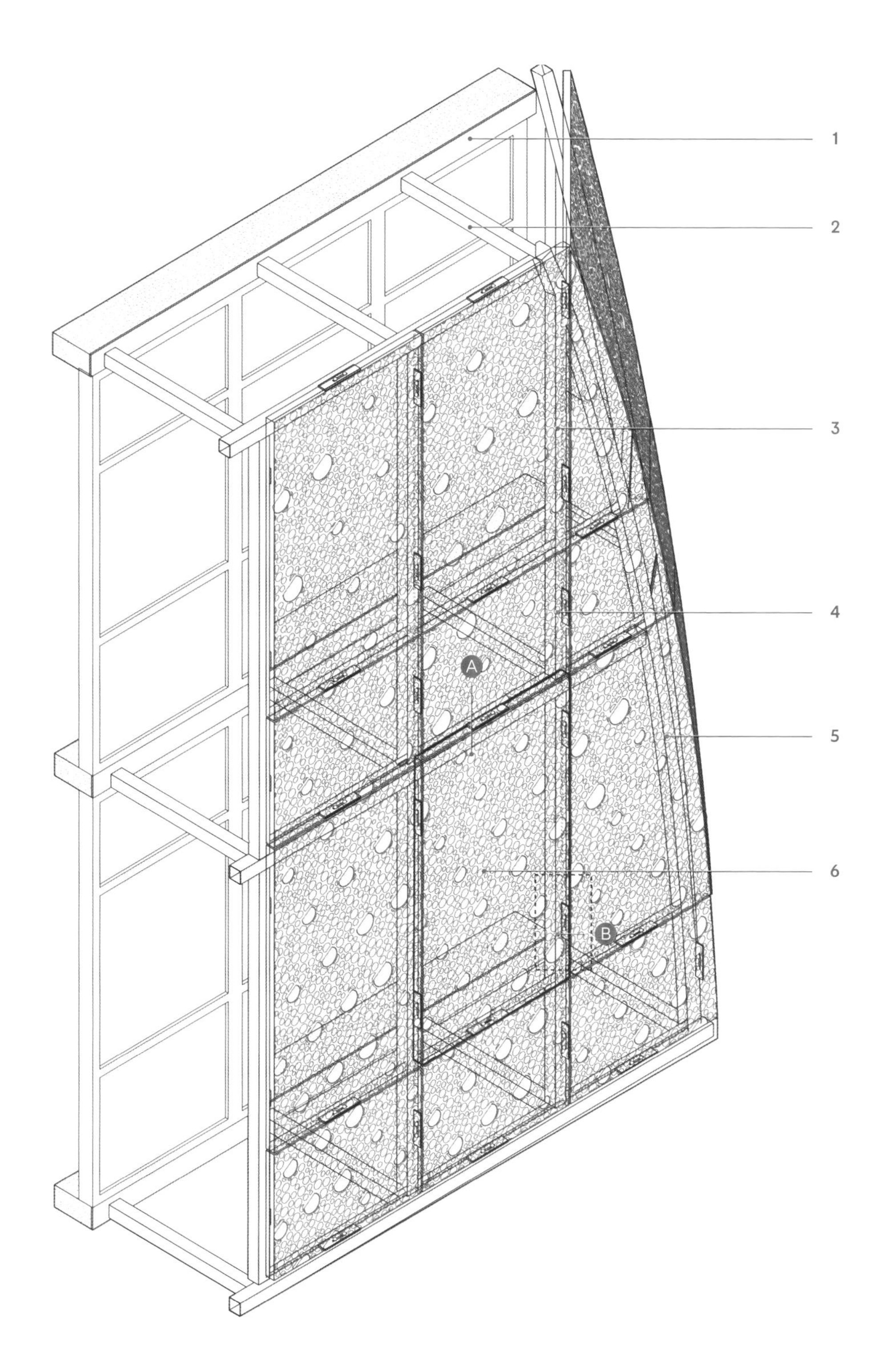

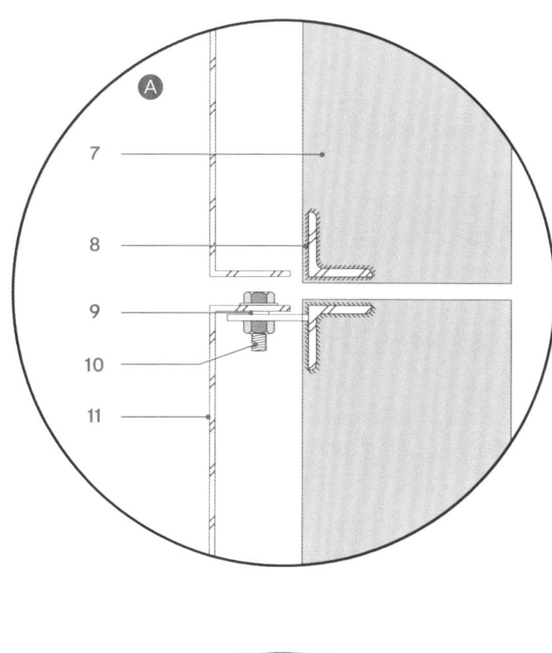

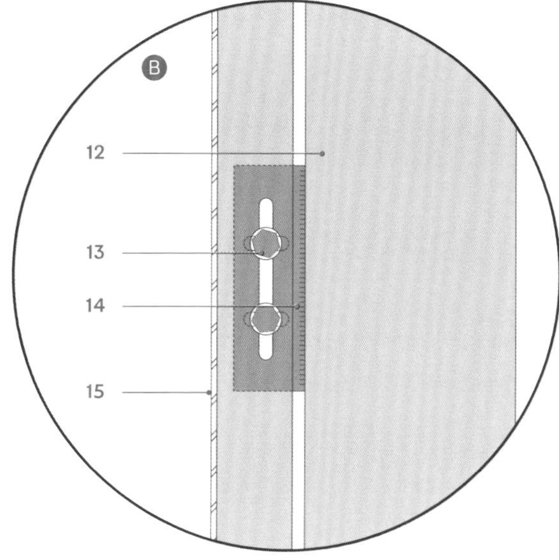

FACADE CONSTRUCTION DETAIL

1 CONTINUOUS STEEL PLATE EMBEDDED IN STRUCTURAL CONCRETE SLAB
2 76MM X 76MM X 3.2MM HSS STEEL TUBE OUTRIGGERS WELDED TO EMBEDDED STEEL PLATE
3 3/16" STEEL CONCRETE PLATE
4 16MM (5/8") BOLTED CONNECTIONS
5 76MM X 76MM X 3.2MM HSS STEEL TUBE FRAME FOLLOWS SHAPE OF FACADE
6 5MM (6 GAUGE) PERFORATED STEEL PANEL

7 76MM X 76MM X 3.2MM HSS STEEL TUBE FRAME
8 2 X 2 X 1/4" STEEL ANGLES WELDED TO HSS TUBE
9 3/16" STEEL PLATE
10 FLANGED 6MM (5/8") BOLT CONNECTION
11 5MM (6 GAUGE) PERFORATED STEEL PANEL

12 76MM X 76MM X 3.2MM HSS STEEL TUBE FRAME
13 FLANGED 6MM (5/8") BOLT CONNECTION
14 3/16" STEEL PLATE WELDED TO HSS STEEL TUBES
15 5MM (6 GAUGE) PERFORATED STEEL PANEL

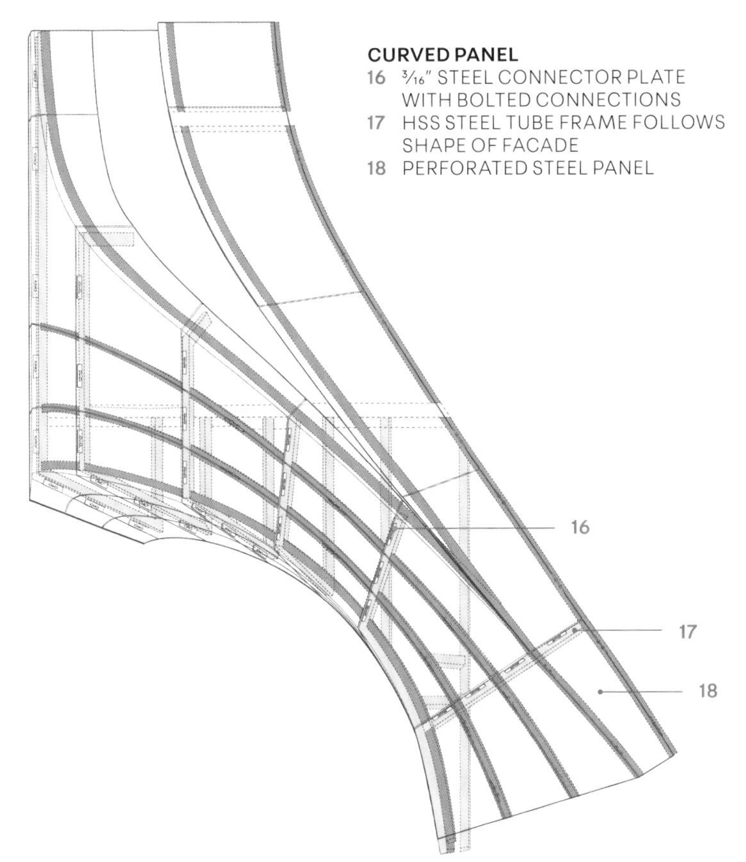

ABOVE TOP AND BOTTOM: Panels are installed on steel framing over an area of the facade that has an extreme degree of curvature.

OPPOSITE AND ABOVE: An elevated, outdoor terrace with a visual connection to the surrounding buildings was created by introducing required open space at the front and side of the building.

53

OPPOSITE: The main building entry occurs at a "tear" in the building's skin.

ABOVE AND FOLLOWING PAGES: On upper levels, the facade screens light into the office interiors and becomes a double skin with an accessible interstitial space, while conjuring an abstract rendering of the city beyond.

LOCAL.MX

ABOVE, OPPOSITE, AND FOLLOWING PAGES:
A perforated facade featuring folded metal
plates produces a field of shimmering tracery.

53

12

Camelback Residence

PARADISE VALLEY, ARIZONA, U.S.A.
2013–2018

The Camelback Residence is a desert oasis set in a suburban neighborhood. The single-story, 10,000-square-foot house rests on a gradually sloping, 2-acre site and is both set back from the street and buffered by generous native landscaping, evoking a sense of isolation. The use of a raw, pared-down materials palette creates a striking juxtaposition to the natural surroundings. At the same time, the building's extreme horizontality and staggered roofs mitigate the desert climate without compromising comfort and use of both the inside and outside.

The plan of the five-bedroom project was developed as a series of parallels that align with the view to a key geological feature in the adjacent mountain range. Each line represents a sequence of spaces running perpendicular to the circulation spine, several of which have a corresponding roof that cantilevers over adjacent outdoor features. These steel elements stretch unobstructed up to 30 feet from the interior and at their widest, span more than 33 feet, adding significant structural complexity to the house. Their staggered heights produce clerestories that, in conjunction with horizontal bands of glazing along the bottom of the 1-foot-deep concrete walls, allow indirect, natural light to penetrate to the core of the plan and create a paradoxical appearance of weightlessness. The cantilevers greatly reduce, and in some cases, eliminate direct sun exposure, minimizing heat gain and protecting the interior from the harsh environment. The roofs strike a balance between providing coverage to large outdoor areas, so that they can be enjoyed more days of the year, and maintaining views from inside the building to the nearby mountains.

FLOOR PLAN
1 ENTRANCE
2 LIVING ROOM
3 DINING ROOM
4 KITCHEN
5 FAMILY SPACE
6 MAIN OFFICE
7 MAIN BEDROOM
8 MAIN BATH
9 CLOSET
10 BEDROOM
11 BATHROOM
12 PLAYROOM
13 CHILDREN'S STUDY
14 GYM
15 UTILITY
16 STORAGE
17 GARAGE

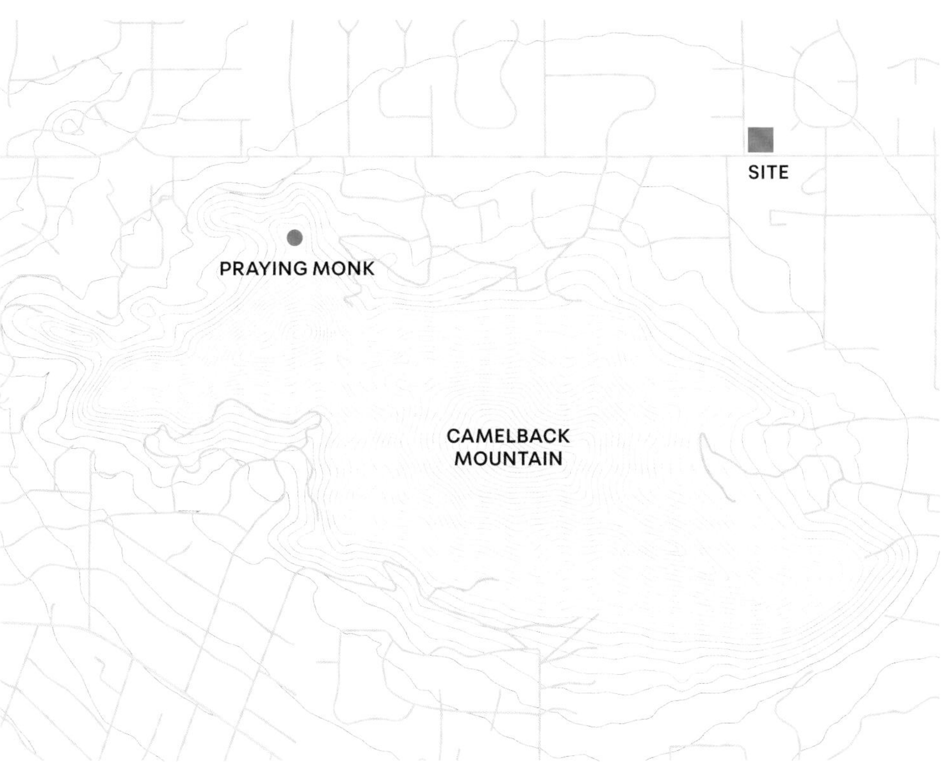

PREVIOUS PAGES: The Camelback Residence's layered spaces and expansive pocket doors allow the procession through the house to oscillate between indoors and outdoors, nature and domesticity.

LEFT: The house's oblique orientation on the site was chosen to direct its primary views toward the Praying Monk, a well-known rock formation resembling a figure in prayer.

ABOVE: Drawn toward the house through its connection to the Praying Monk, the visitor's progression into the home is guided by a series of suspended concrete walls amid the manicured desert landscape.

OPPOSITE AND ABOVE: The home's extensive cantilevering eaves provide protection from the desert sun and create outdoor shaded areas. Beyond this, a sculptural gazebo and firepit provide a quiet and well-shaded space from which to observe the house and contemplate the surrounding landscape.

SECTION AND SUN STUDY

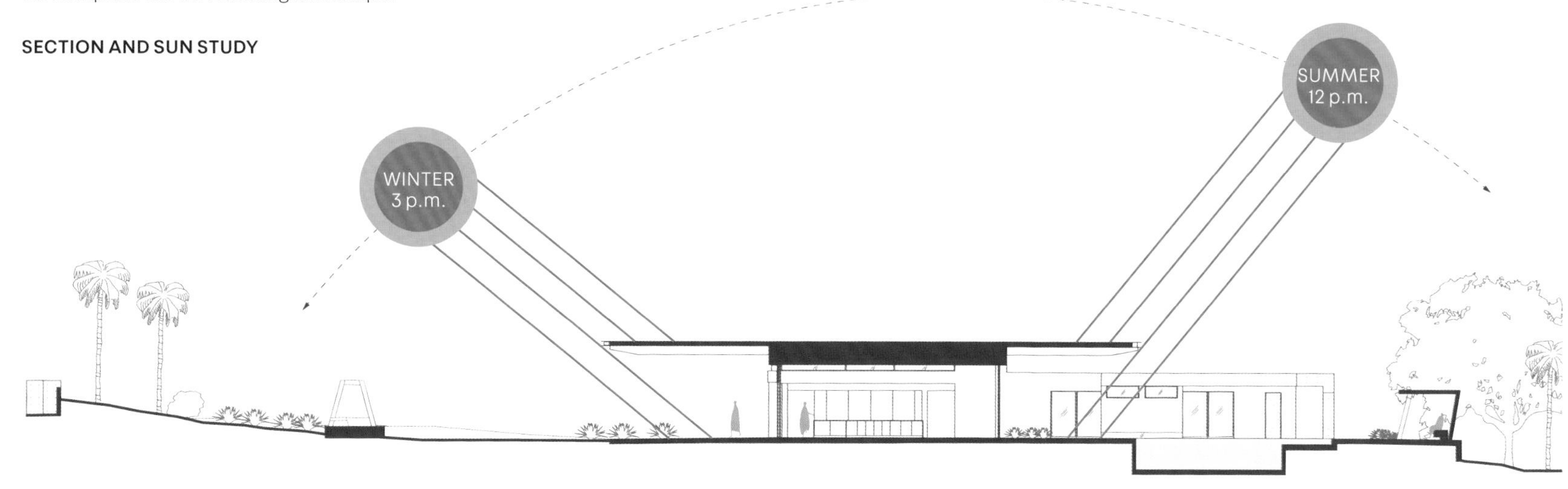

WALL SECTION DETAIL

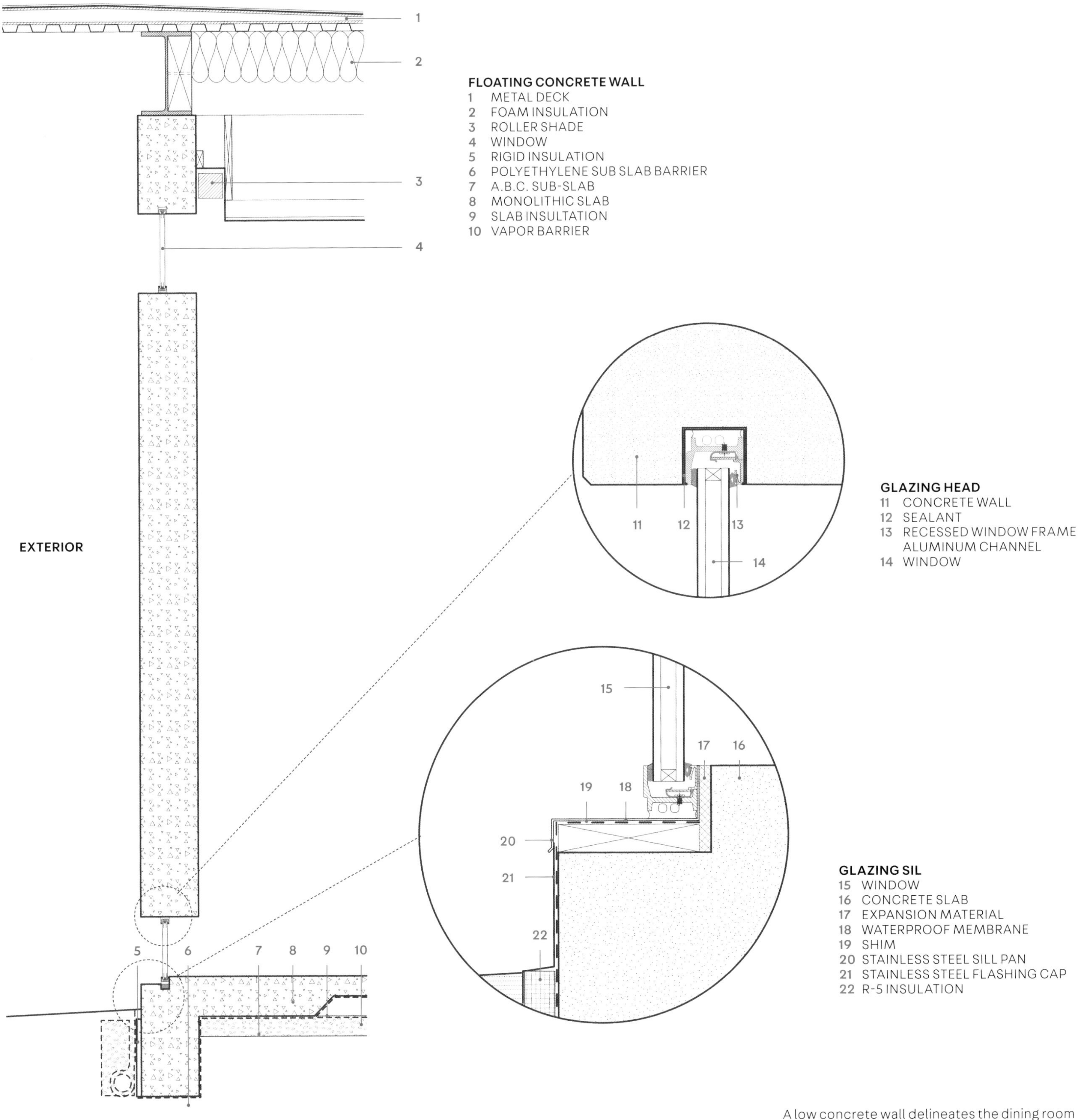

A low concrete wall delineates the dining room from the formal living areas while continuing the material language of the exterior.

OPPOSITE: A procession through the concrete planes provides a curated, gallery-like experience of the house.

ABOVE: Clerestory windows permit natural daylight, which casts dramatic lines throughout the day.

ABOVE: The opening from the kitchen frames the front yard gazebo.

OPPOSITE: Isolated from the other living spaces, the main bath extends to an exterior meditation garden.

ABOVE AND OPPOSITE: Viewed from the house, the gazebo serves as a quiet space to relax.

FOLLOWING PAGES: Surrounded by nature, the house, gardens, and gazebo allow a peaceful lifestyle.

Philippe Samvura
IWitness educator in Rwanda
After completing an IWitness training workshop in Rwanda with an
educator, Philippe Samvura passed the knowledge he learned to othe
Rwanda as an "IWitness Ambassador." Samvura and Marthe Twiney
organized a workshop for their colleagues at Saint-Vincent Muhoza
School. The trainers reported that all participants showed great inter
and acquired knowledge on how to introduce highly sensitive subject
1994 Genocide against the Tutsi in Rwanda to their students.

Jennifer Goss, Robert E. Lee High
School, Virginia

Swipe for More

13

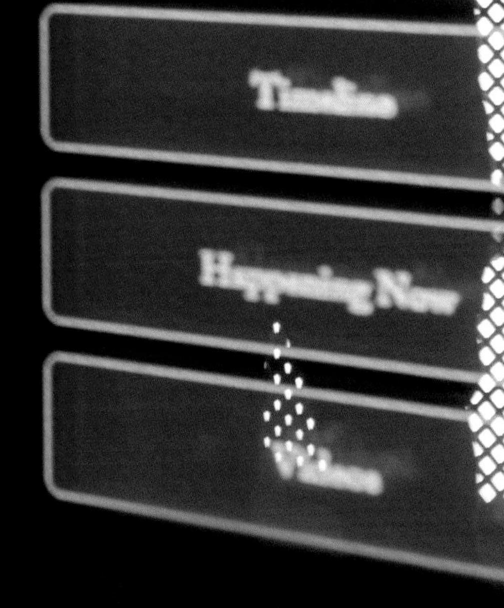

PREVIOUS PAGES: A visitor engages with the full-height, interactive touchscreen along the back wall of the lobby of the USC Shoah Foundation—The Institute for Visual History and Education Global Headquarters.

ABOVE: Due to the open "neighborhood" plan and collective shared spaces, acoustic performance was a major design factor. A dropped, faceted ceiling was coupled with a prefabricated acoustic paneling system to create intimate zones within the open spaces while maintaining high acoustic performance.

USC Shoah Foundation—The Institute for Visual History and Education Global Headquarters

LOS ANGELES, CALIFORNIA, U.S.A.
2015–2019

The USC Shoah Foundation—The Institute for Visual History and Education Global Headquarters is a conduit for this institution's growing collection of more than 55,000 video testimonies by witnesses to genocide, and supports its nearly 100-person staff to realize its mission: "To develop empathy, understanding, and respect through testimony." Located on the top floor of an existing library at the University of Southern California, the 10,000-square-foot project is the institute's first dedicated public space, allowing it to welcome visitors, mount exhibitions, and host events. Designed with deep emotional and cultural sensitivity, the new headquarters is an immersive, didactic environment adapted to the needs of the institution.

Fundamental to the institute's mission is the use of storytelling as a tool to engage and educate. Access points to the institute's archive were integrated with the architecture—glowing pillars and walls with touchscreens, a life-size interactive display, and a new virtual-reality experience—allowing individual and group learning as well as remote content curation. To convey the extent of the institute's operations, a skewed processional corridor has been established for tours, and a faceted dropped ceiling distinguishes circulation space from open work areas, hiding large conduits discovered during demolition and creating a subtle change in floor-to-ceiling height.

A flexible and scalable "neighborhood" organizational strategy was also adopted. Each neighborhood varies in size and geometry but has a central meeting table for collaborative work that eliminates the need for more dedicated meeting space elsewhere. Workstations, with a variety of bench seating, standing desks, and hot desk options, come with a movable cubby of drawers for impromptu one-on-one conversations, and recessed table legs allow desk widths to be adjusted as needed. Overall, neighborhoods are arranged to maximize transparency and connectivity within an efficient framework that is adaptable as future needs emerge.

FLOOR PLAN
1 GRAND STAIR
2 GEORGE AND IRINA SCHAEFFER HALL
3 JONA GOLDRICH CENTER FOR DIGITAL STORYTELLING
4 WELCOME CENTER
5 COMMUNAL PRINT ROOM
6 DISTINGUISHED GUEST SUITE
7 SARA AND ASA SHAPIRO VISITORS LOUNGE
8 COLLABORATIVE MEETING ROOM
9 CENTER FOR ADVANCED GENOCIDE RESEARCH
10 EDITING SUITE
11 TESTIMONY AND INTERVIEW ROOM
12 STORAGE
13 OPEN WORKSTATION
14 NURSING WOMEN'S LOUNGE
15 RESTROOM
16 VISITORS LOUNGE
17 KITCHEN
18 INSTRUCTIONAL AND STUDY ROOM
19 FORMAL MEETING ROOM
20 VIDEO CONFERENCE BOOTHS
21 THINK TANKS
22 EVALUATIONS AND SCHOLARSHIP

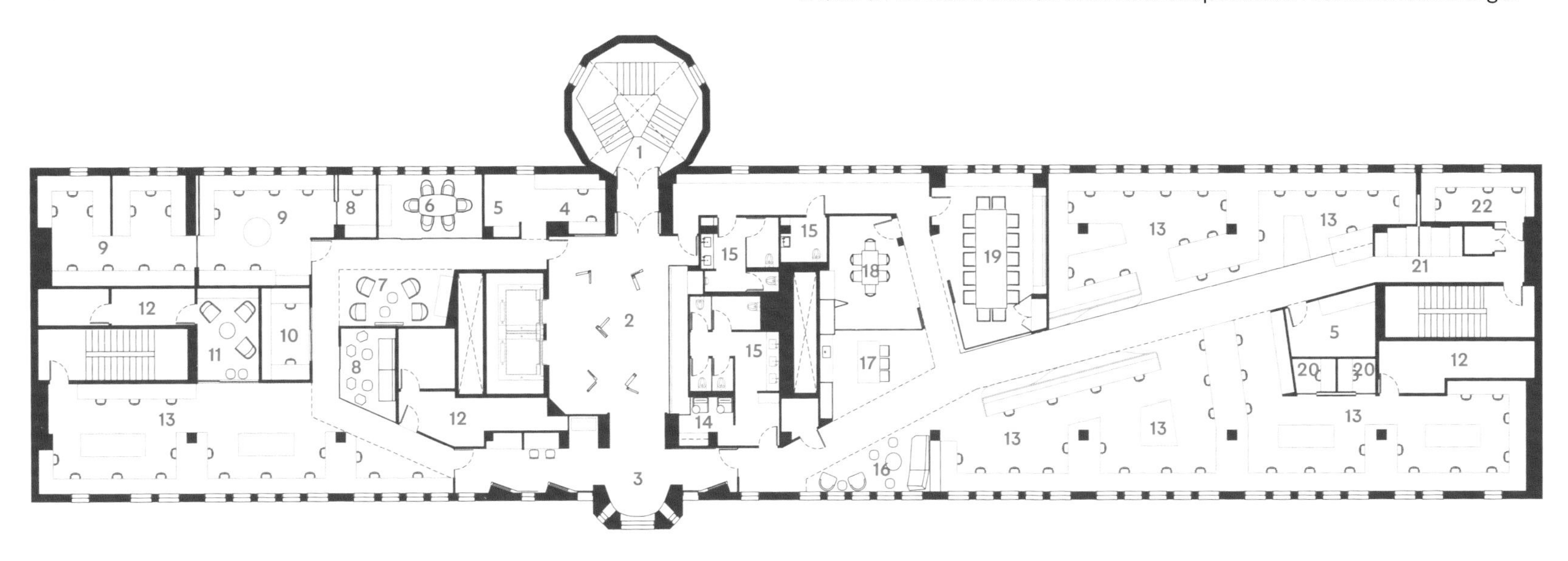

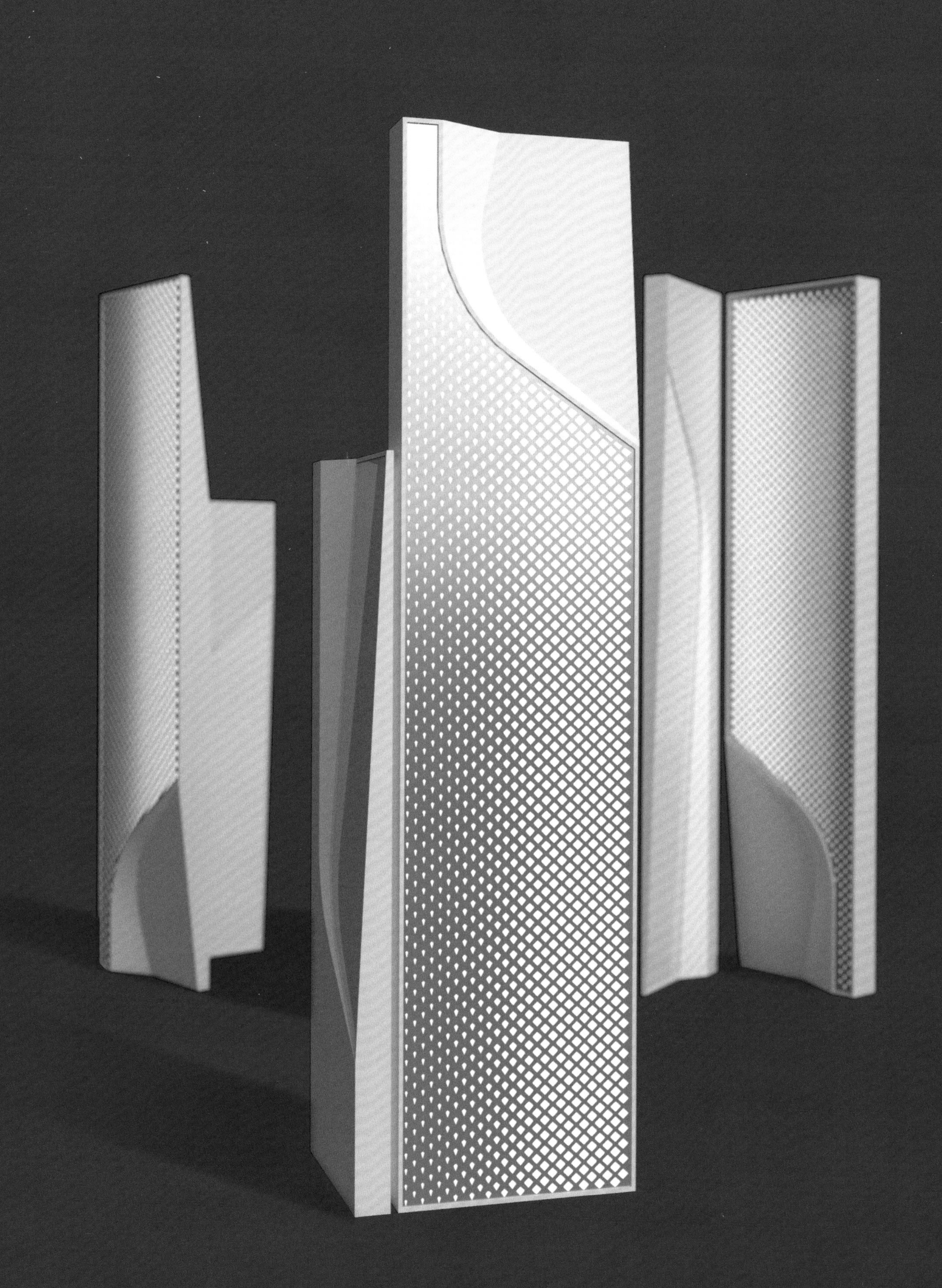

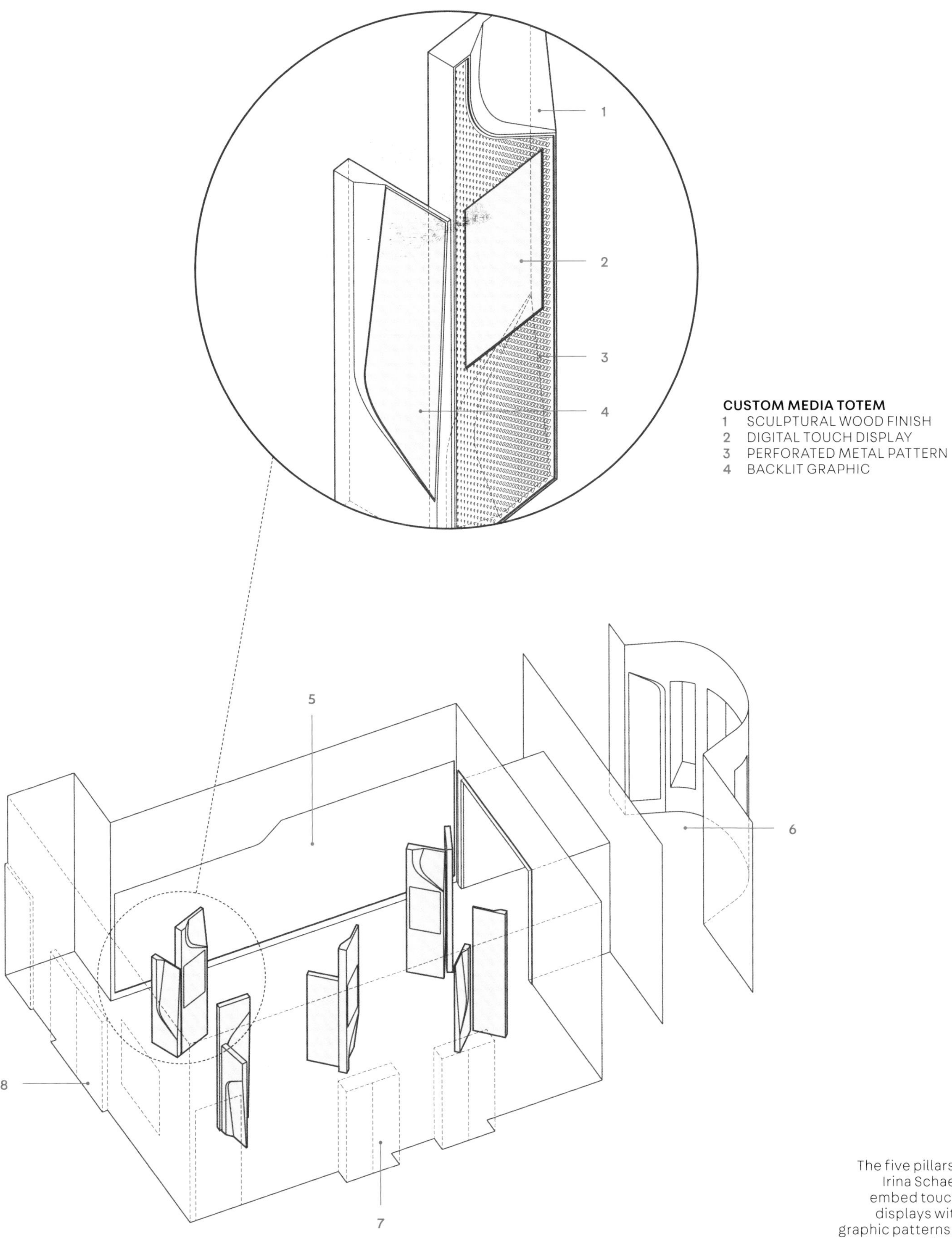

CUSTOM MEDIA TOTEM
1 SCULPTURAL WOOD FINISH
2 DIGITAL TOUCH DISPLAY
3 PERFORATED METAL PATTERN
4 BACKLIT GRAPHIC

SCHAEFFER HALL
5 FULL-HEIGHT DIGITAL TOUCH DISPLAY
6 JONA GOLDRICH CENTER FOR DIGITAL STORYTELLING
7 ELEVATOR
8 GRAND STAIR ENTRY

The five pillars that occupy the George and Irina Schaeffer Hall for Genocide Study embed touchscreens and backlit graphic displays within a language of perforated graphic patterns and subtle wood curvatures, offering an interactive landscape.

ABOVE: A large floor-to-ceiling touchscreen clads the back wall of Schaeffer Hall, allowing for both individual and group engagement with the archival collection.

OPPOSITE: Through their layout, grouping, and articulation, the pillars foster personal engagement with the content. This singular experience is heightened by the darker environment, which immerses the visitor in the stories being shared.

"Victimization and genocide
perpetrated and denied in one
part of the world can become
the breeding ground for greater
crimes against humanity in
another part of the world. It
was my responsibility to
ducate and inform so that
istory won't be repeated."
Michael Hagopian
"Human rights are universal.
Truth is universal. The right
to life is universal."

JONA
GOLDRICH
CENTER
FOR DIGITAL
STORYTELLING

OPPOSITE: Upon leaving Schaeffer Hall, visitors emerge into a brightly lit rotunda with a view of the USC campus beyond. Here the visitor can engage with the institute's content, bringing their shared experience to others. A metal sculpture tells the story of survivor and benefactor Jona Goldrich's life.

ABOVE: Past the rotunda are the Visitors Lounge and the workspaces, each delineated by shifting ceiling planes.

ABOVE AND OPPOSITE: A sliding door system that nests into closets allows rooms to be closed off or reconfigured to be completely open.

Programmatic needs requiring a mix of spaces of varying scales, flexibility, and adaptability were the driving forces in the design.

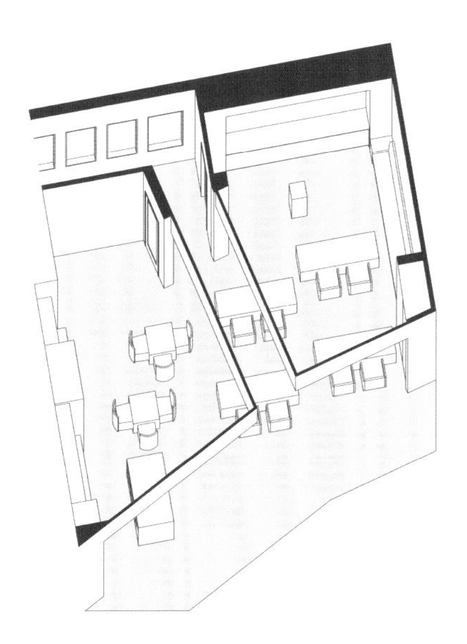

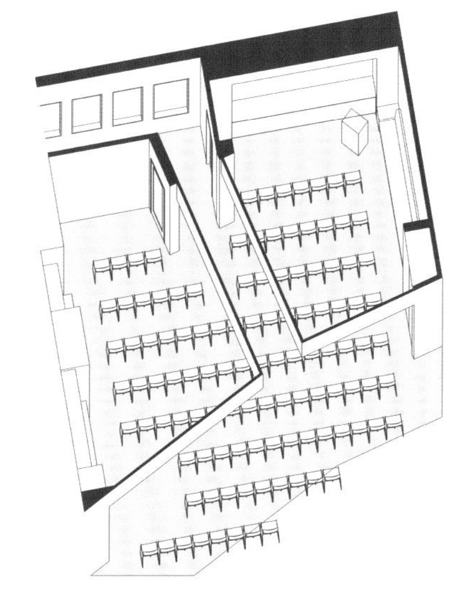

OPPOSITE, ABOVE, AND FOLLOWING PAGES: Workspace areas flow out from a main circulation highway. Custom millwork provides privacy for the desks behind it while also creating a breakout meeting space.

REFLECTED CEILING PLAN

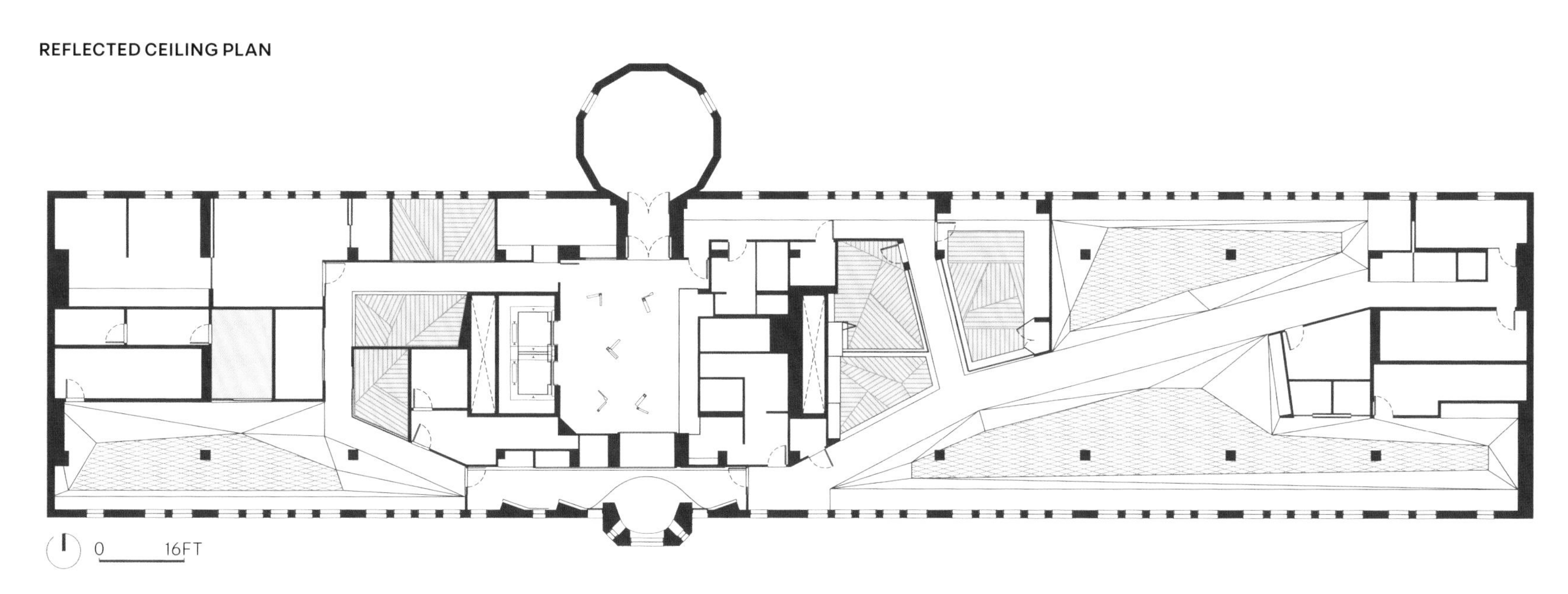

LEADING CHANGE
We bring

The institute's rich and diverse archive is open and accessible yet allows for deeply personal connection as well.

BAR

14

BAR Center at the Beach

LOS ANGELES, CALIFORNIA, U.S.A.
2013–2021

The BAR Center at the Beach has a long history of serving the community and senior citizens in the area. The original two-story dance hall was built in 1923 along the Venice boardwalk. However, after sustaining damage in the 1994 Northridge earthquake, the second floor had to be removed. The renovation and expansion of the remaining structure reimagined the center as a state-of-the-art, intergenerational space, creating a sustaining connection to its surroundings and the community it serves.

The existing single-story 3,500-square-foot building was functionally obsolete, with limited accessibility. The new layout has reorganized the first floor to include an interactive lobby and ocean-facing community room; reinstated the second story, with collaborative spaces, a Jewish multimedia library, and an expansive roof-deck; and added a third floor to house a three-bedroom, two-bathroom apartment. Collectively, these spaces are flexible and designed to accommodate programming for seniors and youth alike.

The facade balances a desire for the center to be welcoming and open to the beach view, and the need for safety and security. A geometric motif based on an abstraction of the Star of David was developed into a metal panel system that is coated with anti-graffiti paint and allows for easy replacement and repairs. The pattern is carried over to the oceanfront facade's glazing, which allows transparency to passersby along the boardwalk.

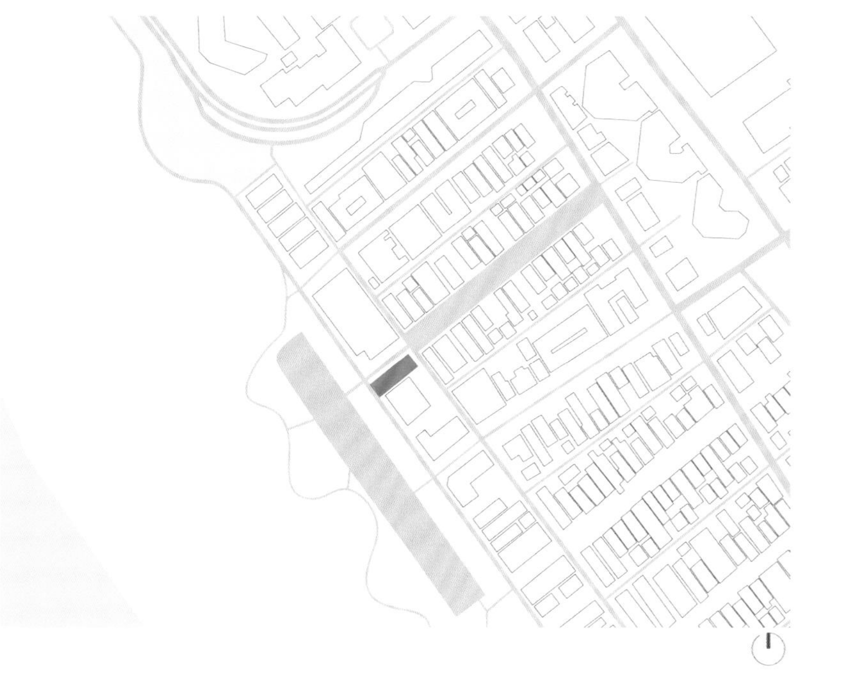

PREVIOUS PAGES: The BAR Center's facade is powerfully abstract in scale yet invites curiosity and engagement through its pattern and assembly.

OPPOSITE AND RIGHT: The center is sited on California's Venice boardwalk, with a lively pedestrian promenade in front and the beach just beyond.

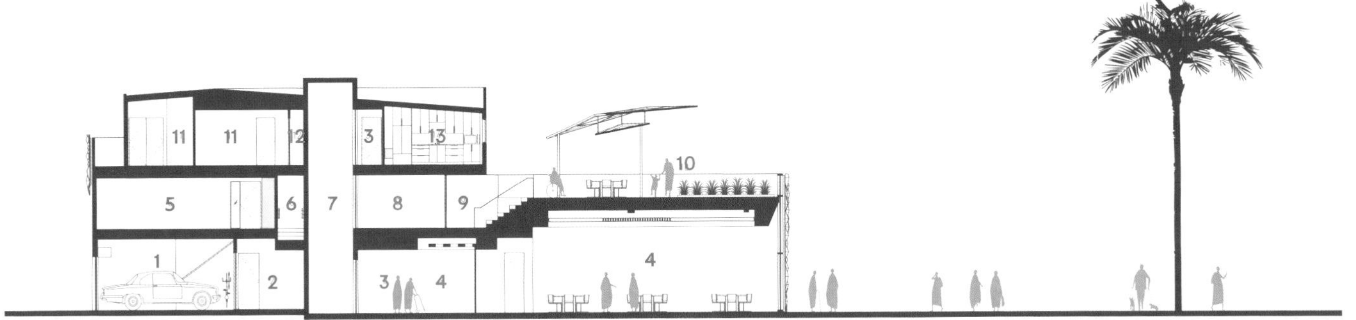

SECTION
1 GARAGE
2 EQUIPMENT ROOM
3 CIRCULATION
4 COMMUNITY ROOM
5 ADMINISTRATIVE
6 STAIR
7 ELEVATOR
8 ELEVATOR LOBBY
9 LOWER DECK
10 OUTDOOR DECK
11 BEDROOM
12 CLOSET
13 LIVING ROOM AND KITCHEN

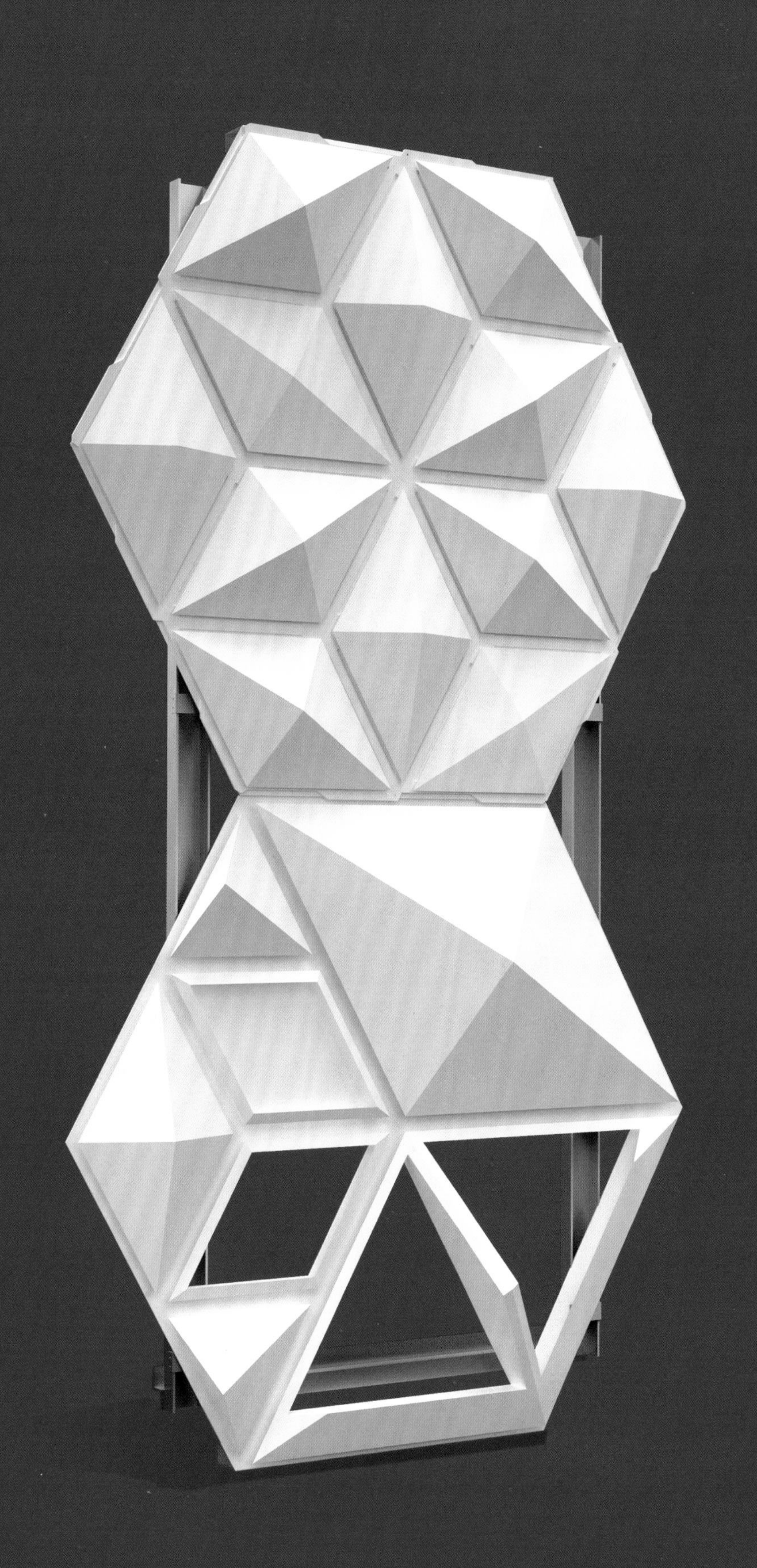

PANEL WALL ASSEMBLY
1 FORMED METAL PANEL
2 ADJUSTABLE STANDOFF
3 VERTICAL CHANNEL
4 EDGE TRIM
5 Z EXTRUSION
6 CONCRETE MASONRY WALL

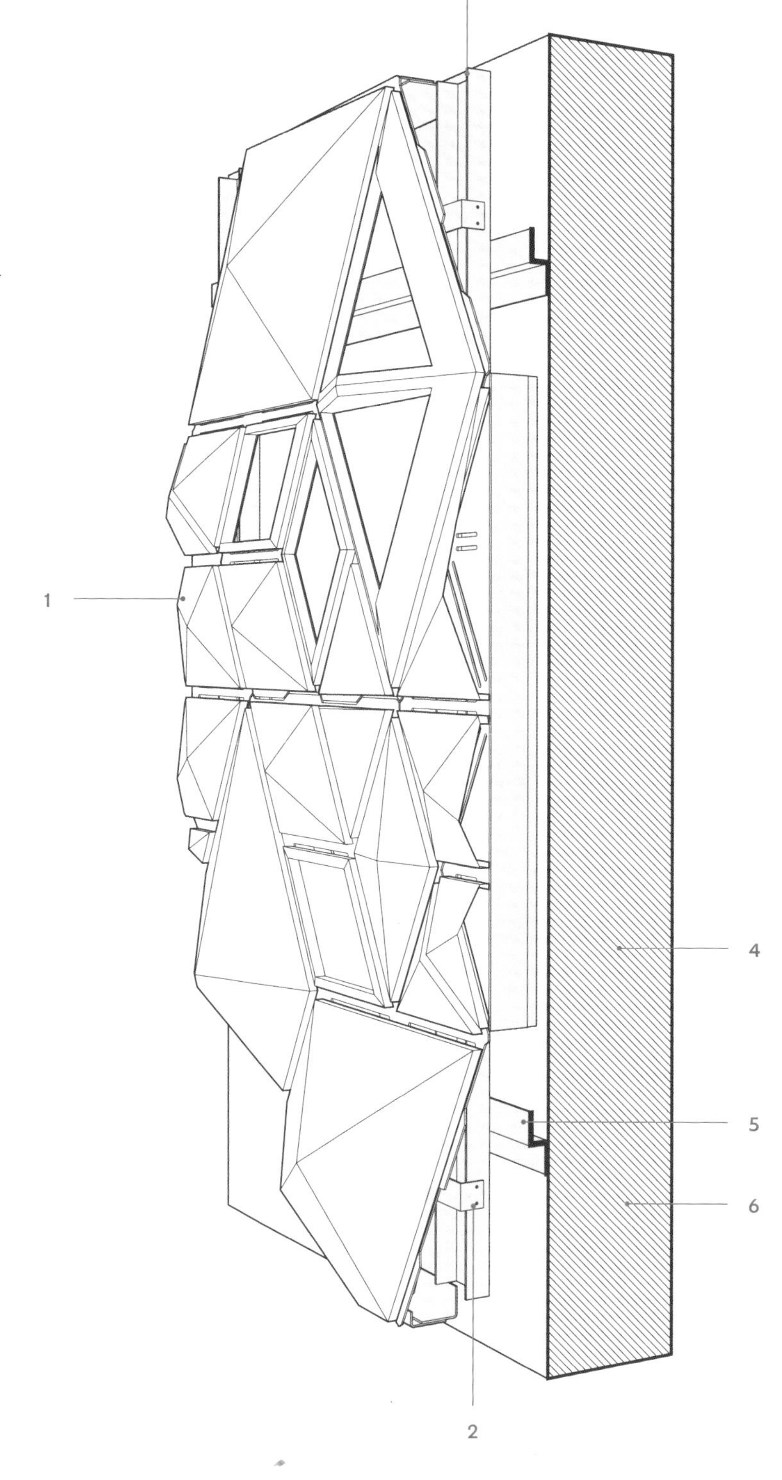

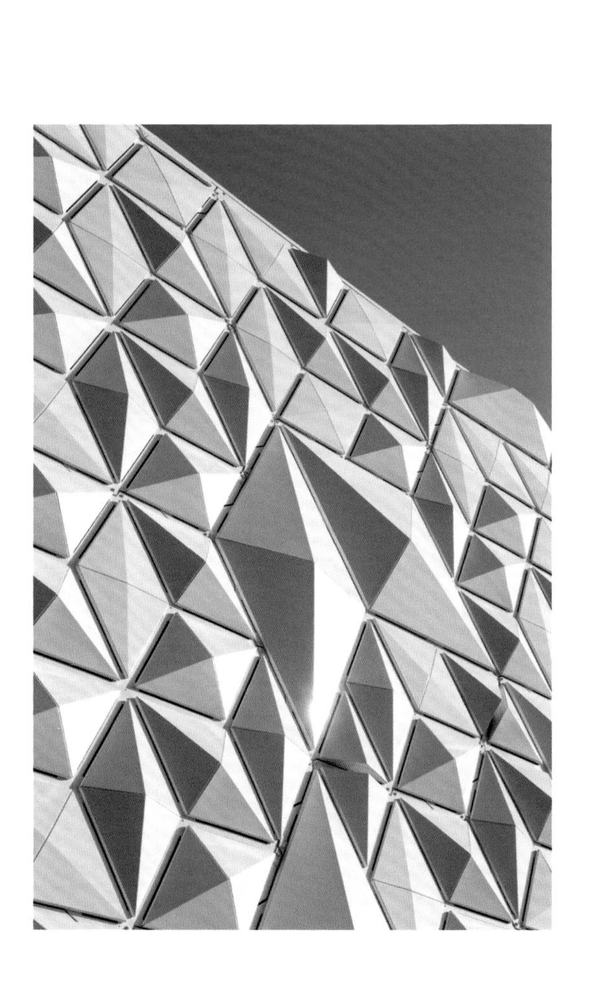

A detail of the metal panel facade, which is the result of a series of abstractions of the geometric system.

The geometric metal panels turn the corner between adjacent elevations, punctuating a material palette involving Jerusalem stone, ceramic tiles, stucco, and laminated glass.

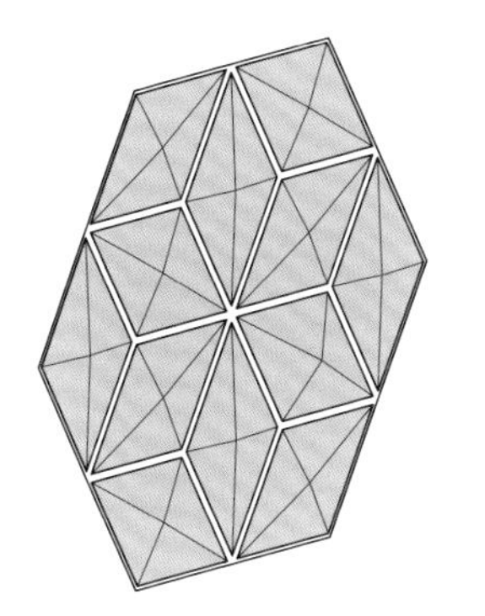

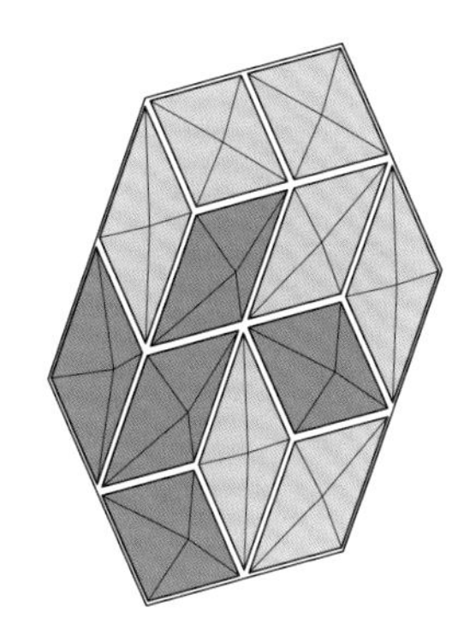

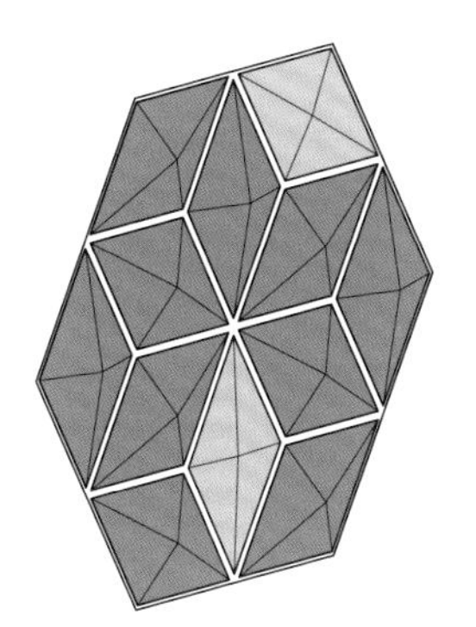

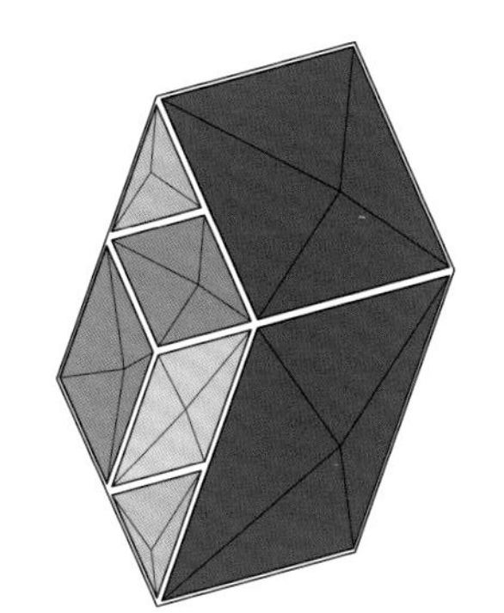

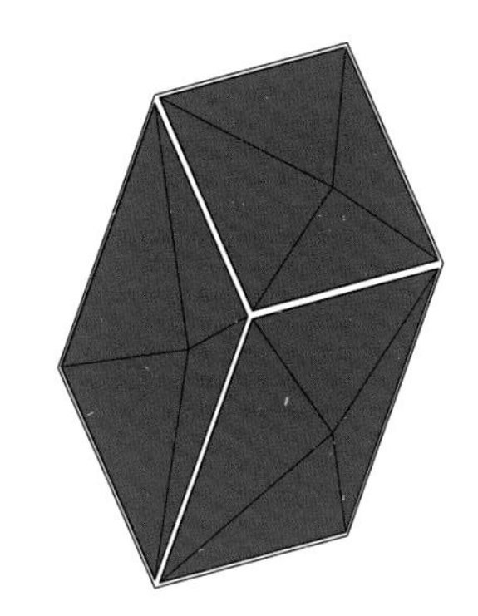

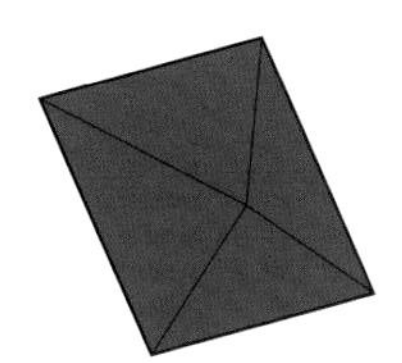

Height of Panel: 6″

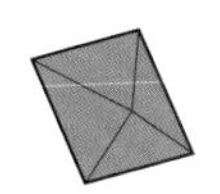

Height of Panel: 4″

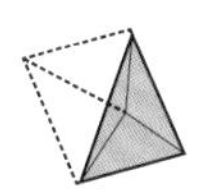

Height of Panel: 4″

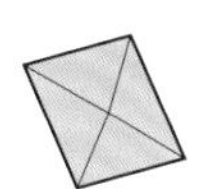

Height of Panel: 2″

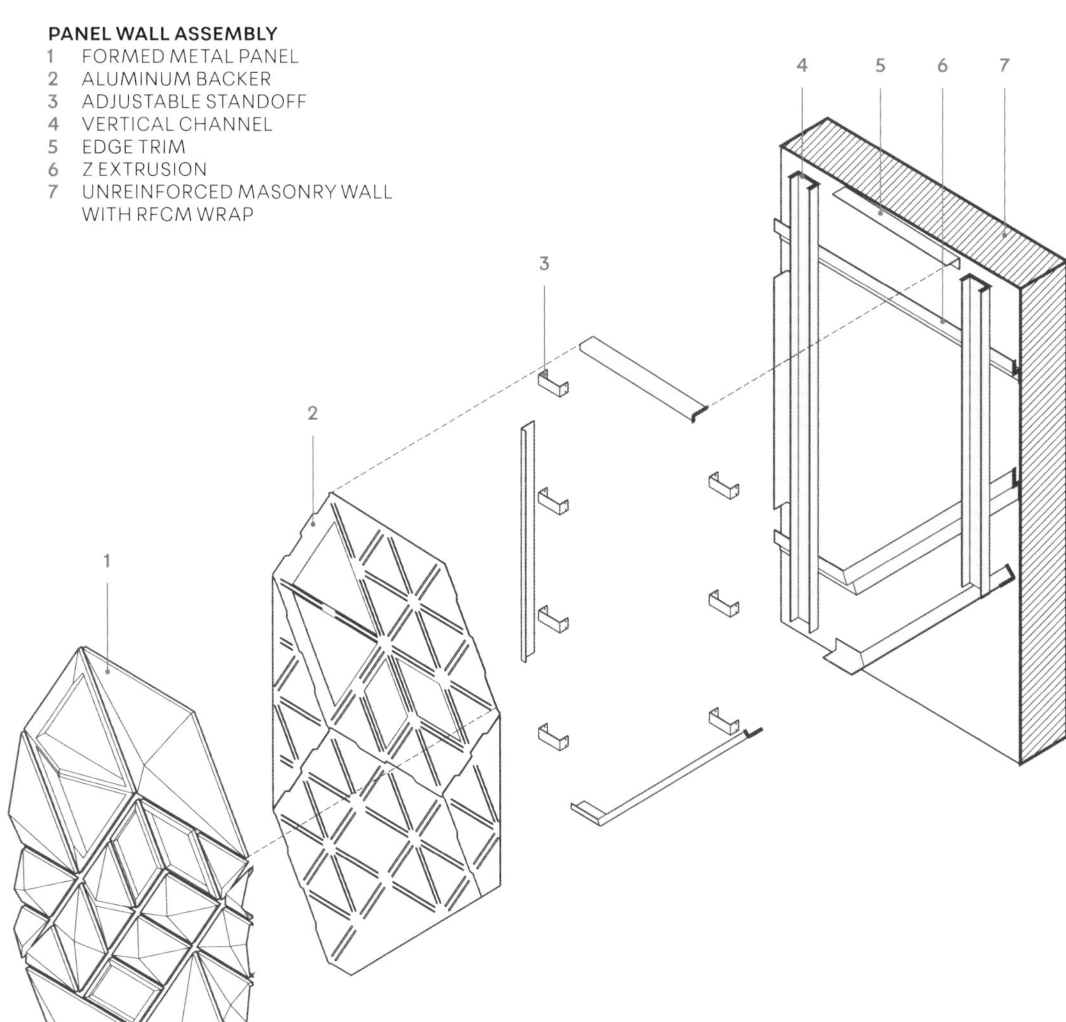

ABOVE: The powder-coated metal panel assembly clips onto a secondary metal sub-panel, which attaches to the existing masonry wall.

BELOW: The geometric pattern's ever-changing scales and articulations transition seamlessly onto the pattern-laminated glass boardwalk facade.

OPPOSITE: The facade transforms throughout the day based on sun location, often taking on the greens and violets of the sky at sunset.

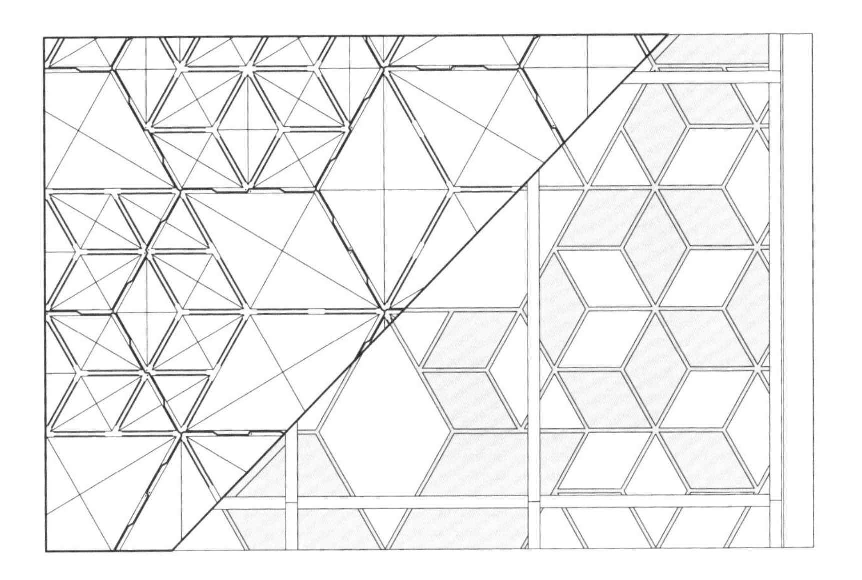

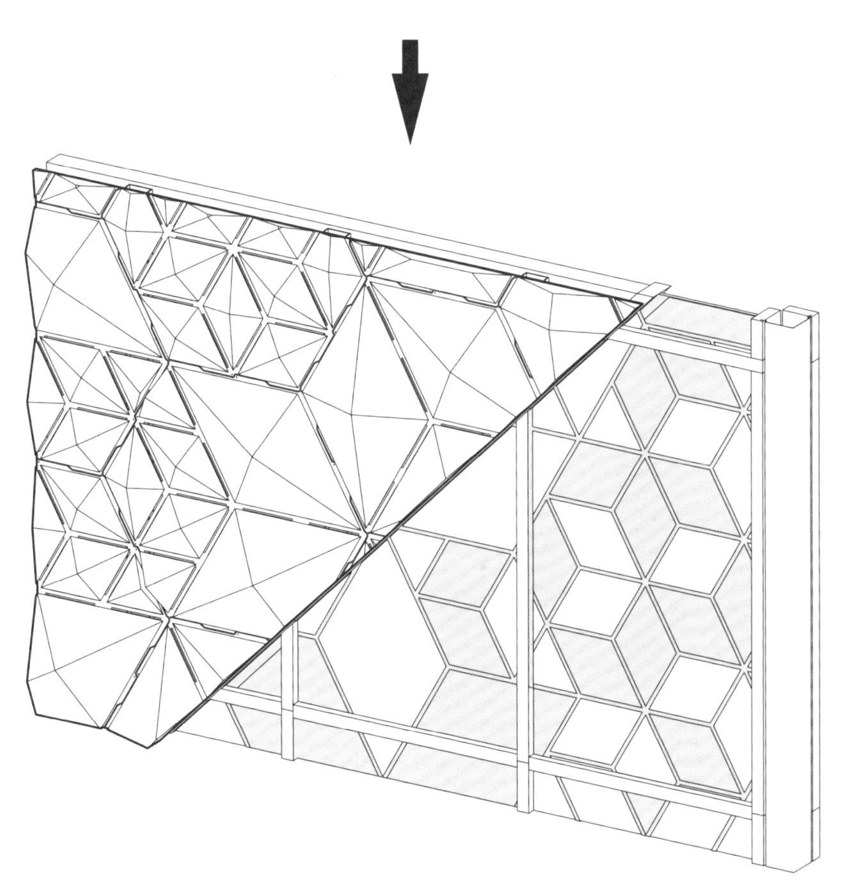

OPPOSITE AND ABOVE: The multifunctional community space with high ceilings and floor-to-ceiling glass is deeply connected to the beachfront site. The suspended baffle system provides robust acoustic performance through its unique pattern.

OPPOSITE TOP: From the deck, visitors can take in the breathtaking ocean views. Generous shade and multiple lounge configurations provide space for myriad events and leisure activities including weddings and Shabbat dinners.

OPPOSITE BOTTOM: A custom trellis, fabricated from three densities of perforated steel panels, provides cover to the deck.

ABOVE: The second floor features bi-folding doors that fully open to the exterior deck. Terraced seating can be used for lectures, presentations, and leisurely gatherings.

The center's illuminated three-dimensional facade is punctuated with large slabs of slanted Jerusalem stone that form the building's entry.

CORDOBA

15

PREVIOUS PAGES AND ABOVE: The Apertures building, illuminated from within at dusk or seen in bright daylight, creates an ever-changing experience on this block in Mexico City.

RIGHT: A section of the building reveals an atrium that cycles light and air vertically through the interior.

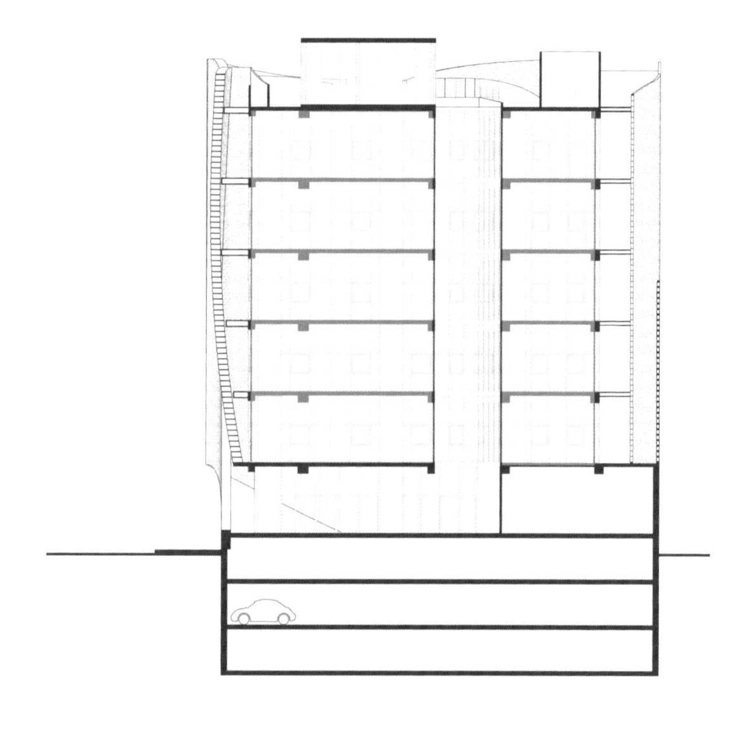

FIRST FLOOR

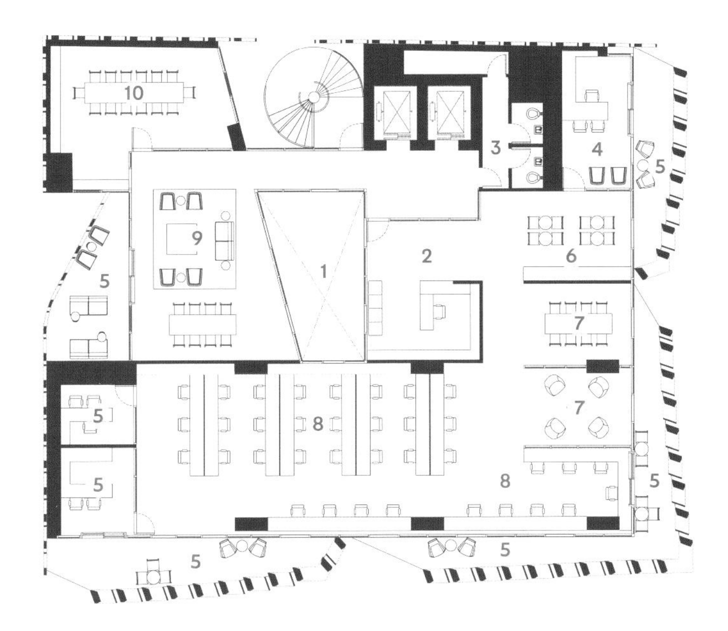

FIFTH FLOOR

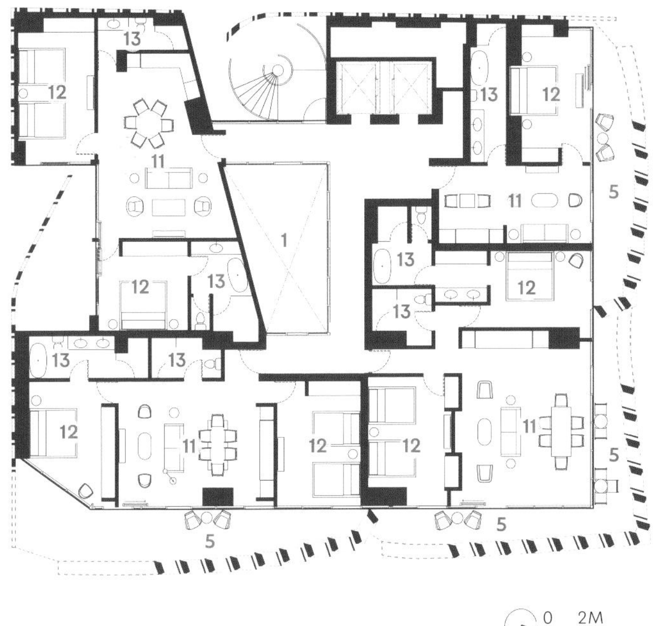

PLANS
1 ATRIUM
2 RECEPTION
3 RESTROOM
4 PRIVATE OFFICE
5 BALCONY
6 KITCHEN
7 MEETING ROOM
8 OPEN OFFICE
9 LOUNGE
10 CONFERENCE ROOM
11 LIVING ROOM
12 BEDROOM
13 BATHROOM

Apertures

MEXICO CITY, MEXICO
2015–2021

Masonry has a long and rich history in Mexico City. Its contextual appropriateness and relative ease of installation led to an investigation of its potential use in the construction of Apertures, a new six-story mixed-use building in the historic Roma Norte neighborhood. The project comprises a restaurant, shared lobby, one level of offices, four levels of hospitality suites, a communal roof-deck, and three levels of subterranean parking. Its outward expression is rooted in a creative approach to the program and local building codes and features a dynamic facade of "sails"; these porous screens protect the balconies, provide privacy, and shape views while curving on two planes and tapering as they touch down at street level. In order to use masonry for the facade and achieve the seismic resilience needed, a new masonry unit and assembly system were developed.

The true innovation in the design of Apertures is unseen. The masonry facades incorporate vertical columns of C-shaped plates embedded into each block and bolted together with only two nuts. These continuous metal columns remove the necessity for grout, mortar, and rebar, and enable the entire assembly to flex as a mesh under lateral force. The use of mechanical fasteners changes the nature of the masonry construction, while the "C" shape of the reinforcing columns allows both transparency through individual blocks and a double curvature (lateral and vertical). The new system aesthetically liberates masonry construction and has enabled the facades of Apertures to exceed the seismic requirements and realize the project's vision.

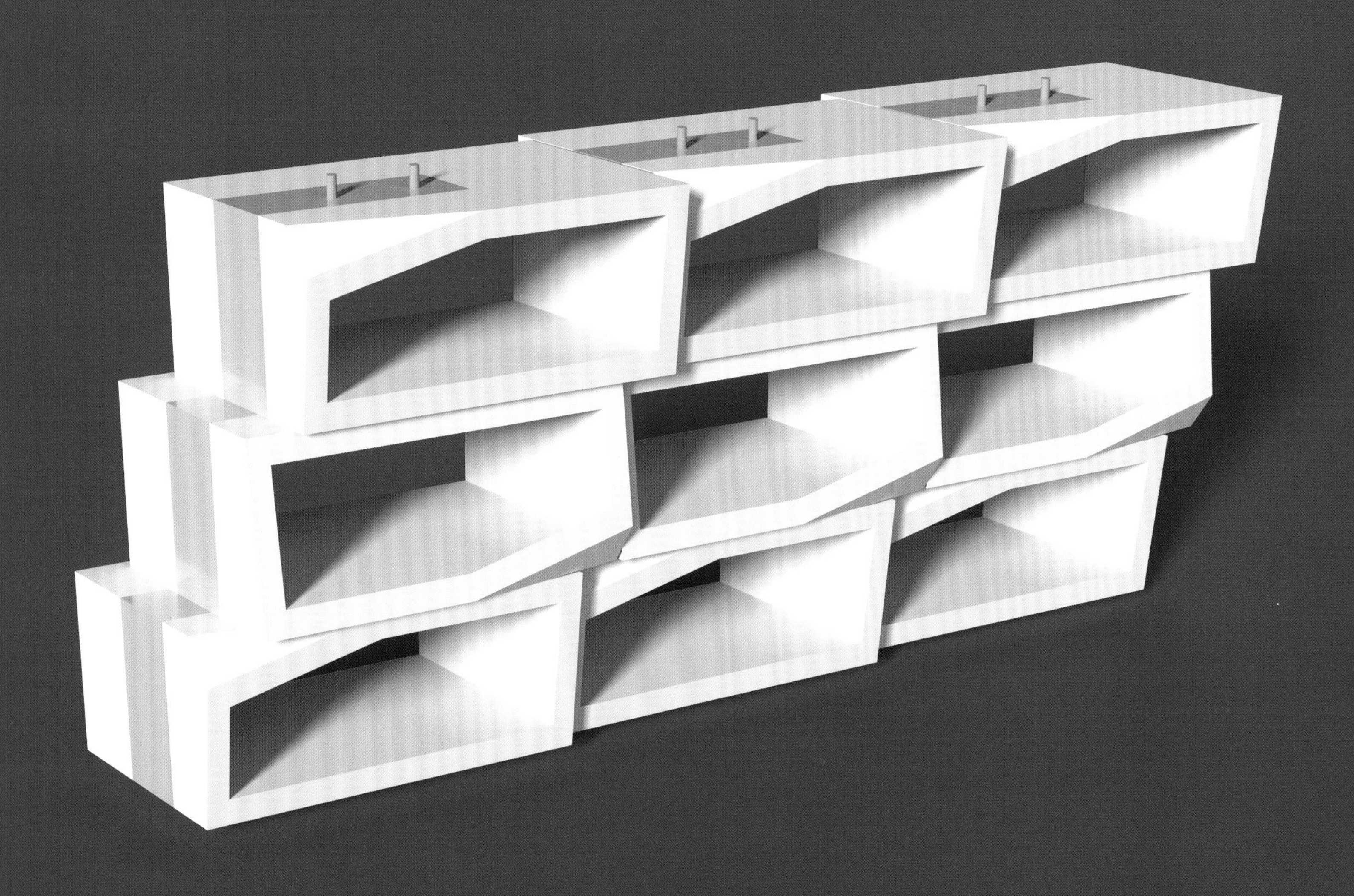

UNROLLED BLOCK FACADE

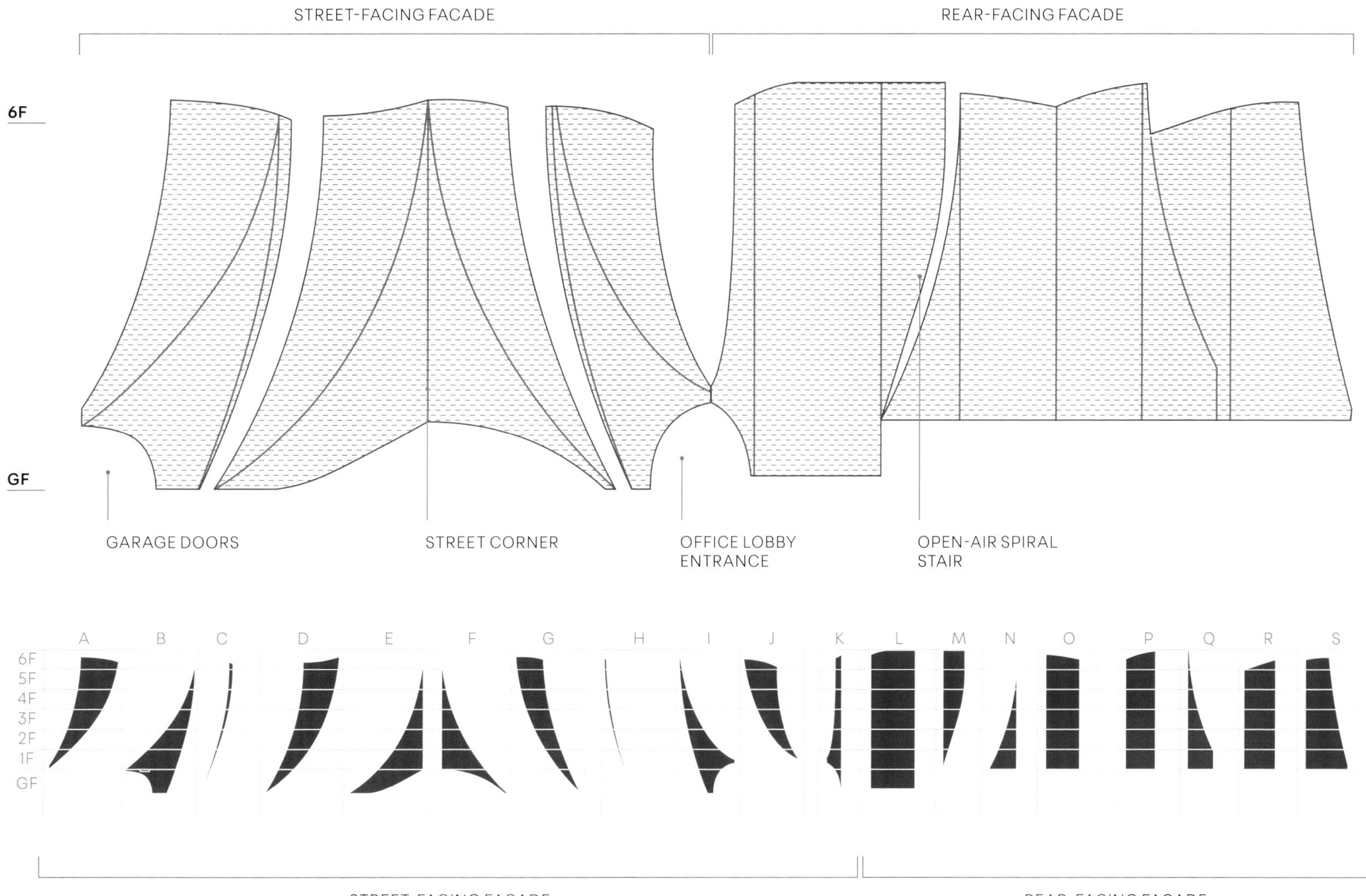

The facade is conceived as a series of "sails" that are horizontally segmented at each floor level. The sails are choreographed to create openings at the street level.

SINGLE BLOCK COMPOSITION

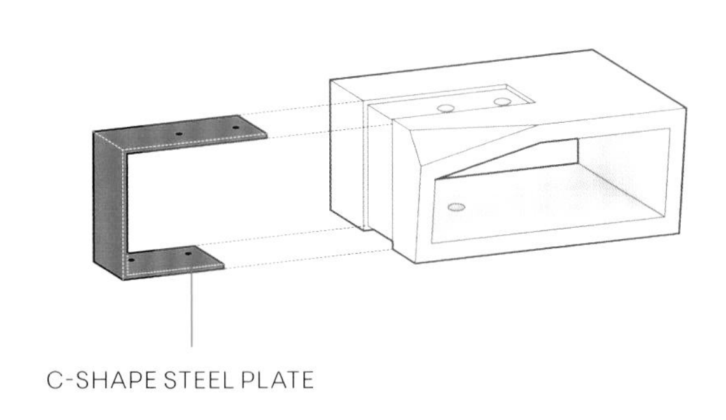

STACKED BLOCK COMPOSITION

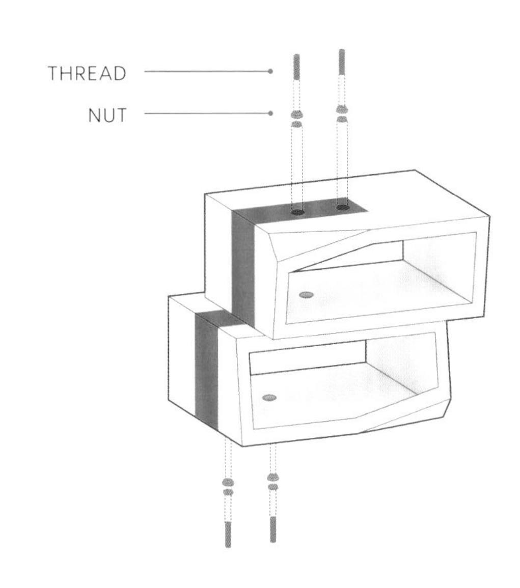

CORNER BLOCK COMPOSITION

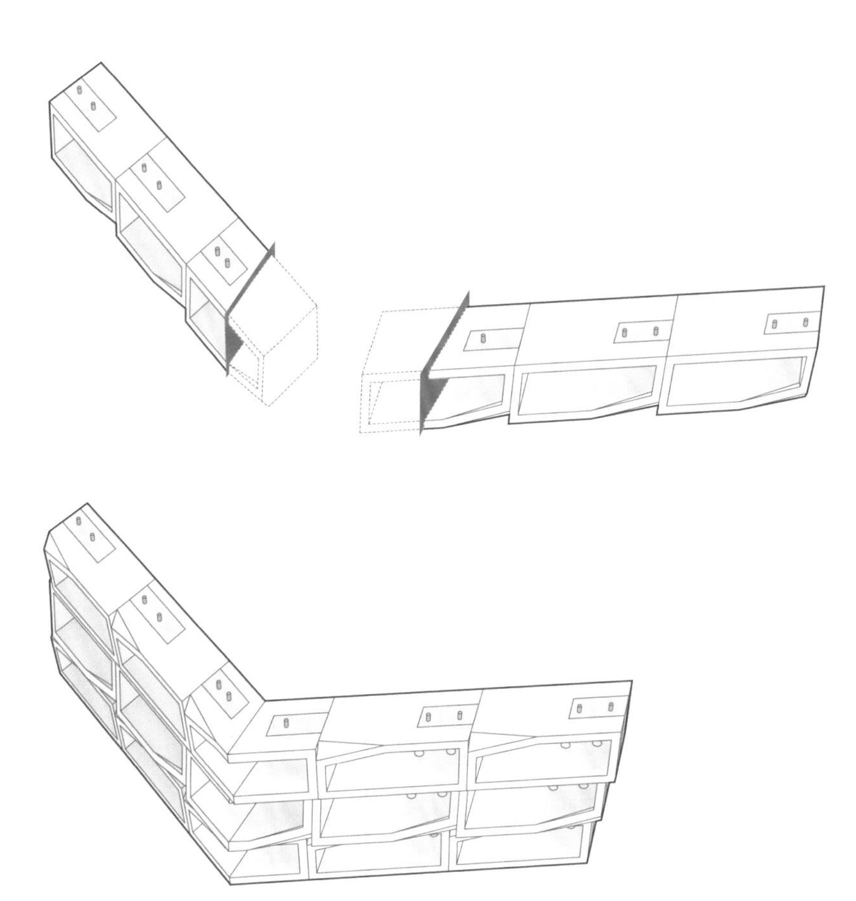

OPPOSITE: A standard block with an integrated reinforcing plate predrilled for bolted connections was conceived for the facade.

ABOVE: The block could be miter-cut in the field into custom blocks for unconfined corners.

BLOCK ASSEMBLY AND STRUCTURE

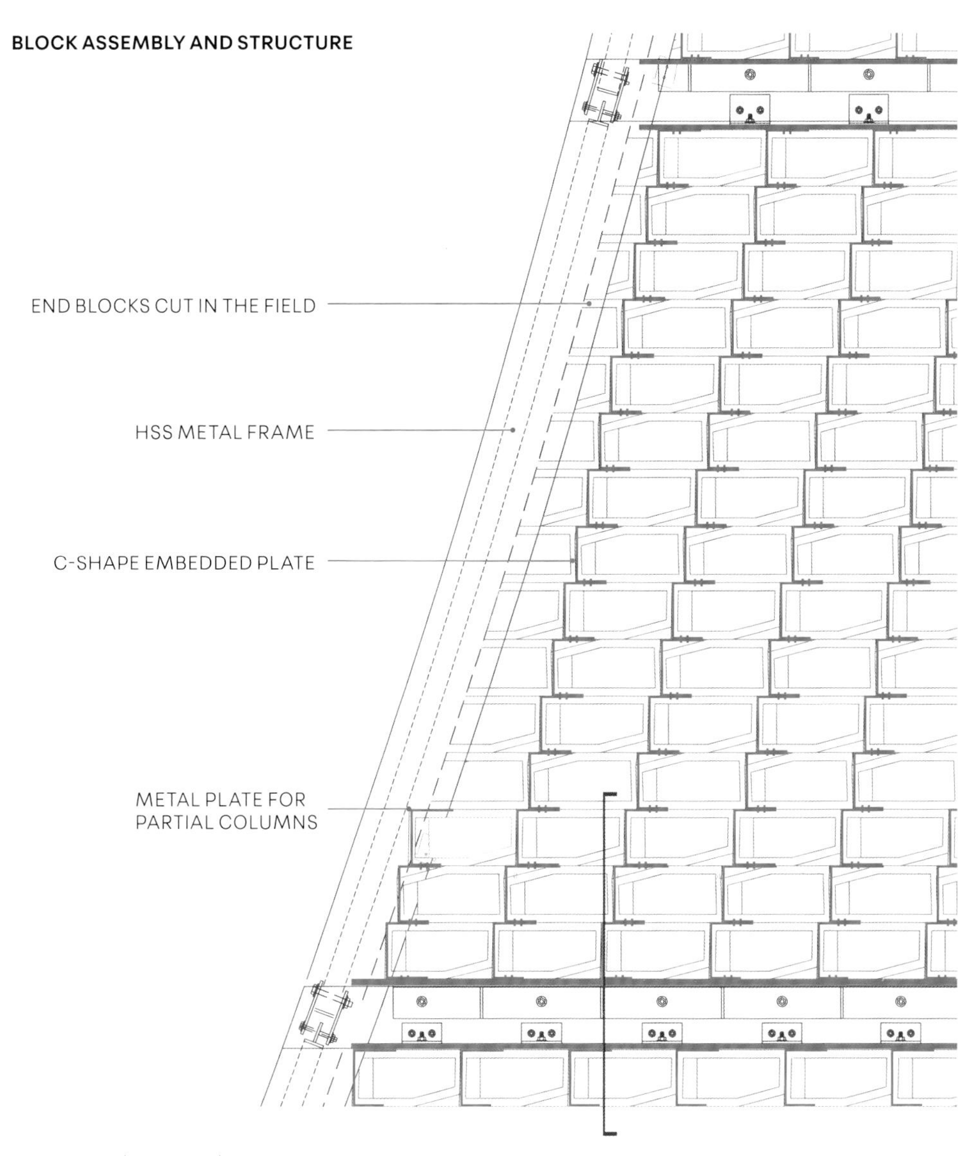

RIGHT: Continuous steel reinforcing columns are attached to top and bottom shelf plates (BELOW) at each floor level.

FACADE-TO-SLAB CONSTRUCTION DETAIL

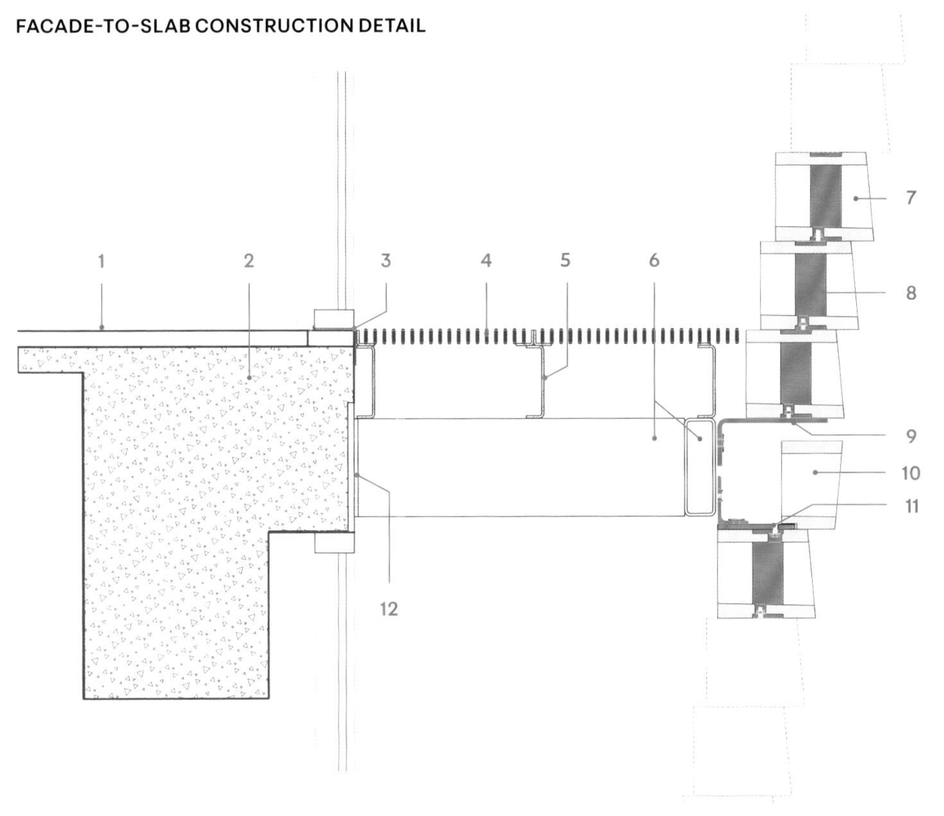

SECTION DETAIL

1 FINISH FLOOR
2 CONCRETE SLAB
3 STAINLESS STEEL FLASHING PAN
4 PAINTED METAL GRATE
5 METAL FRAME CHANNELS
6 HSS TUBE OUTRIGGER
7 FACADE BLOCKS
8 C-SHAPE STEEL PLATE
9 TOP BENT STEEL PLATE
10 FILLER BLOCK
11 BOTTOM BENT STEEL PLATE
12 EMBED PLATE AND ANCHOR BOTS

BUILDING SECTION AT BALCONY

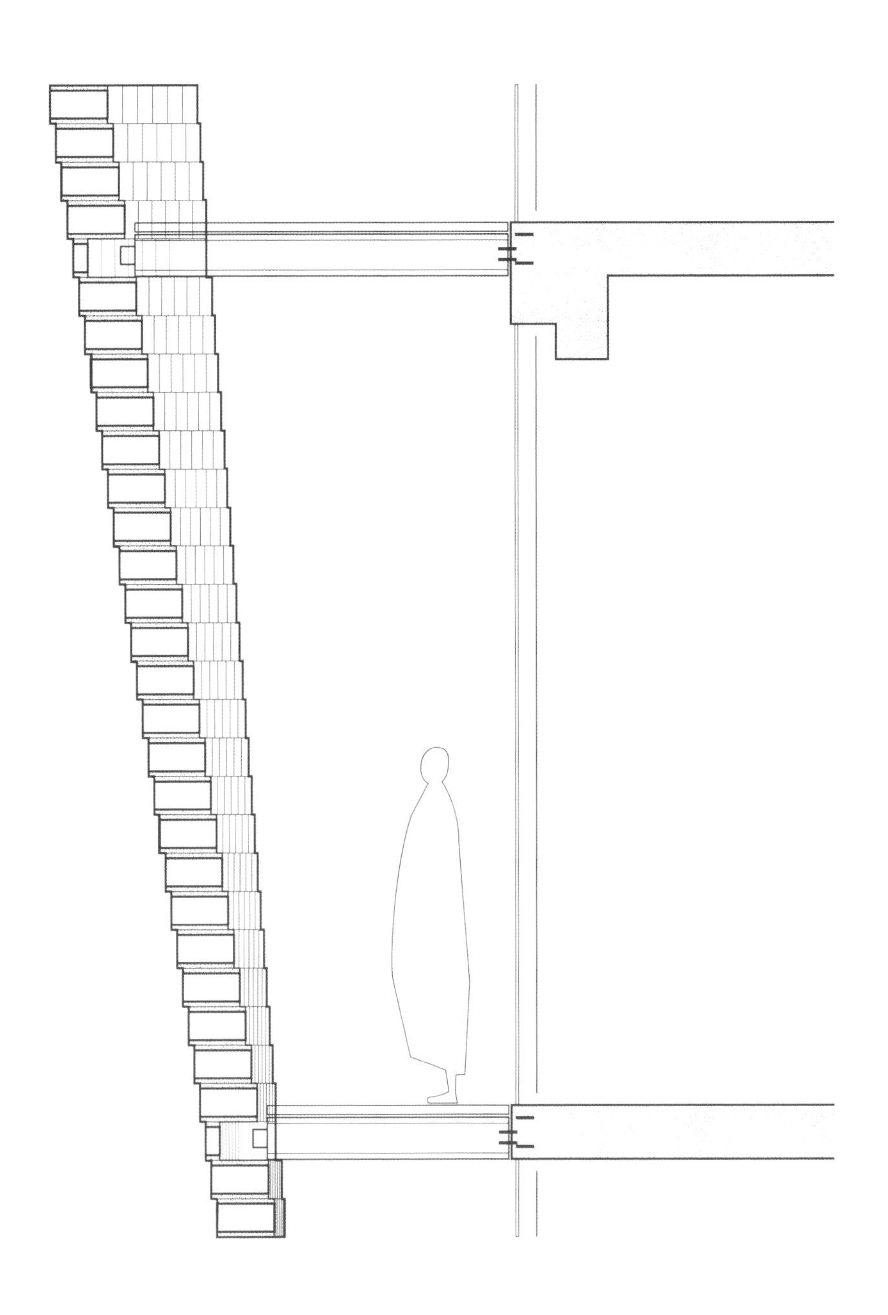

BELOW: The brick assembly was tested for resistance against several seismic and structural factors.

The block-screen sails screen light while also revealing unobstructed views of the city.

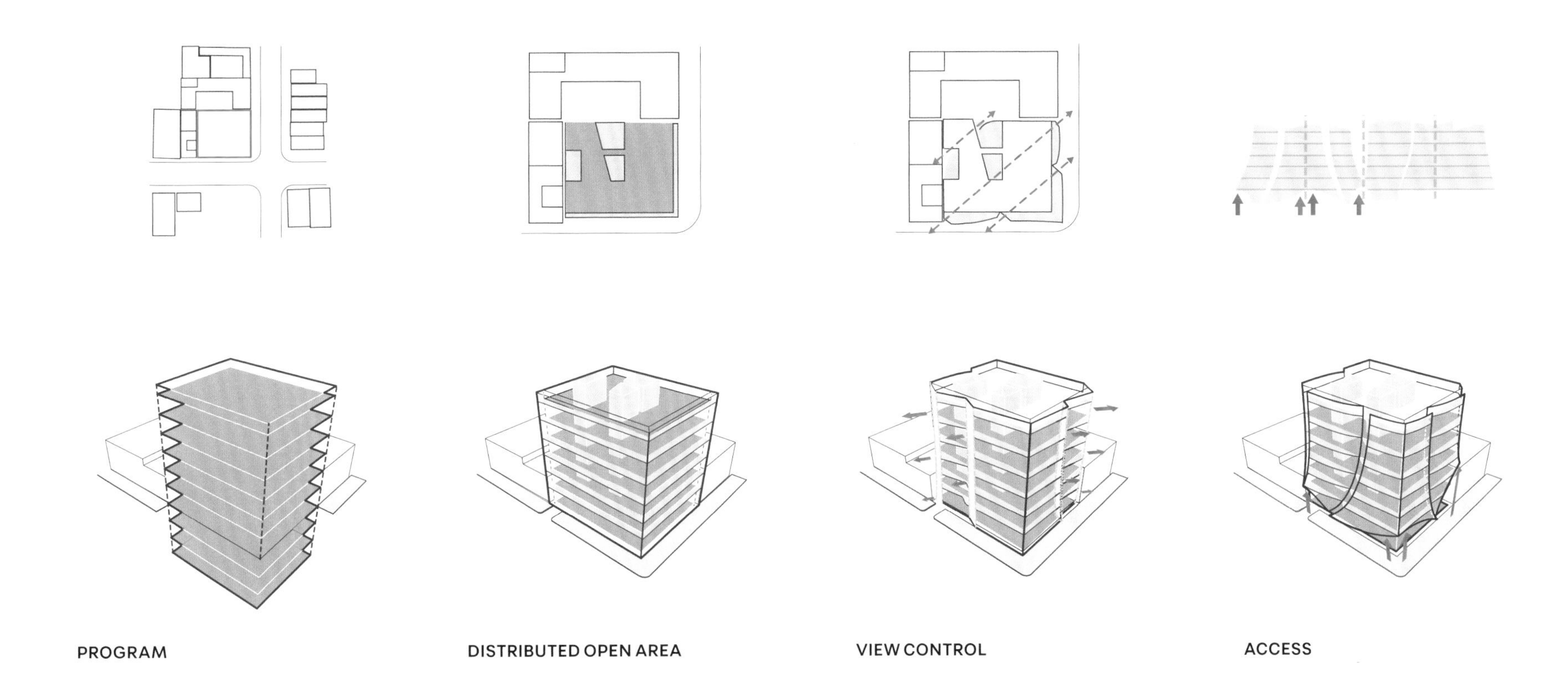
PROGRAM
DISTRIBUTED OPEN AREA
VIEW CONTROL
ACCESS

CORDOBA

BELOW: The entrance lobby translates the qualities of the exterior—curved sails assembled from geometric blocks—into a warm interior experience.

OPPOSITE: A view across the atrium reveals the layering of solid, void, glass walls, and block sails.

A typical apartment offers screened views of the city. The double-skin creates open-air balconies between the block sails and the glass exterior walls.

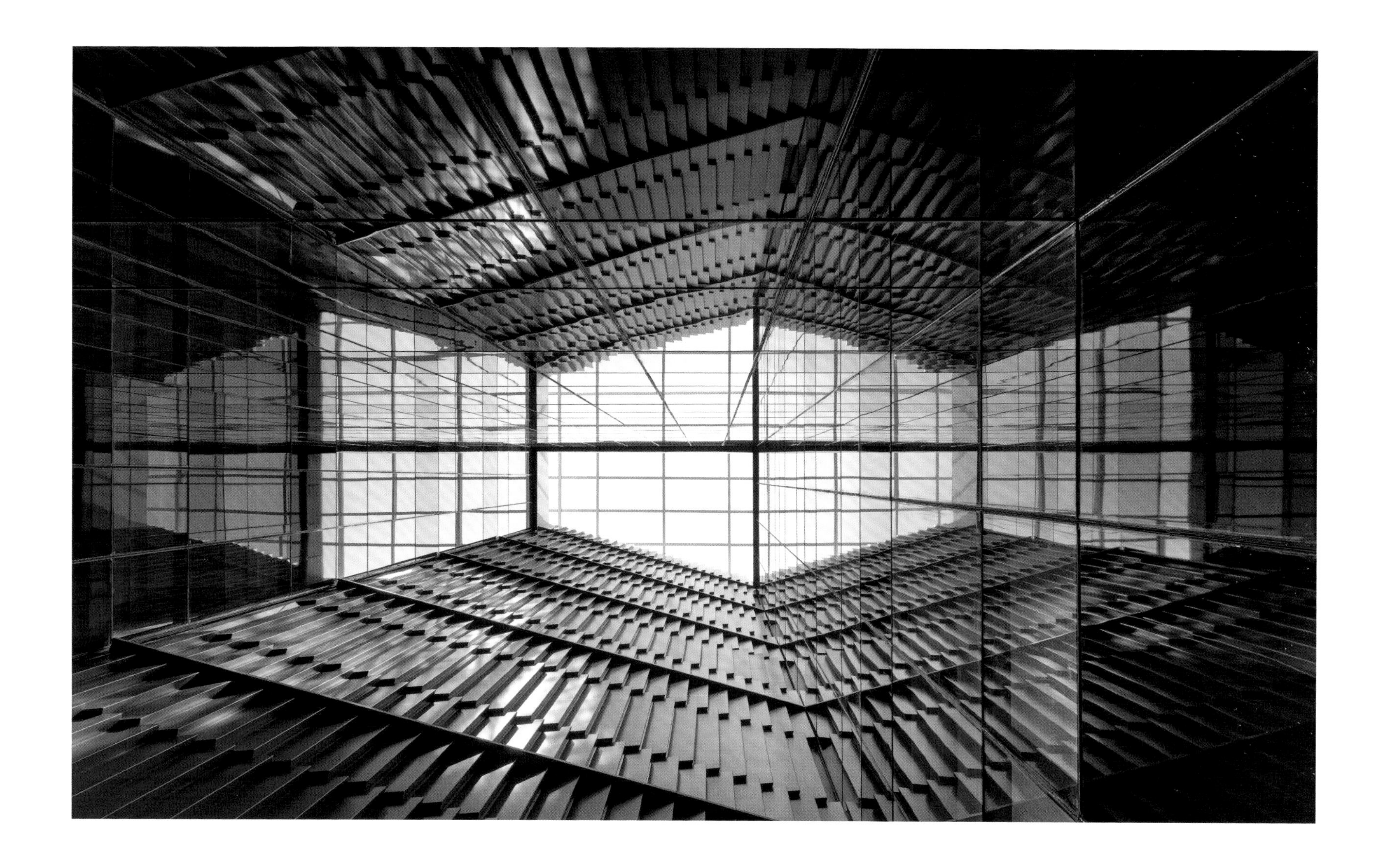

ABOVE: A geometric wall system descends from the side of the atrium and becomes a backdrop to the reception area.

RIGHT: An open-air spiral staircase is partially veiled within the sails of the facade.

In the lobby, guests and residents are presented with a material palette that reinterprets the language of the exterior facade: the sail shapes are echoed in a curved ceiling and the angular quality of the blocks is recalled in a geometric wall application.

The sails surpass typical residential stacking by giving the balconies privacy and individual character.

LEFT: A detail of the block system shows the play of light and shadow on the geometric assembly.

FOLLOWING PAGES: At dusk, the building appears as a lantern in the skyline.

Project Chronology

Flint Peak Residence
Pasadena, California
1997

Pagani
West Hollywood, California
1998

Mataja Residence*
Malibu, California
1999

Huell Howser Desert Installation
Twentynine Palms, California
2000

Nick + Stef's Steakhouse
Los Angeles, California
2000

Weissberg Residence
Beverly Hills, California
2000

Kinara Spa
West Hollywood, California
2001

Moomba
Los Angeles, California
2001

Patina on Melrose
Los Angeles, California
2001

Patina at Walt Disney Concert Hall
Los Angeles, California
2003

America West Arena Restaurant
Phoenix, Arizona
2003

Café at Walt Disney Concert Hall
Los Angeles, California
2003

LA Phil Store at Walt Disney Concert Hall
Los Angeles, California
2003

Ahmanson Founders Room
Los Angeles, California
2006

**Belzberg/Wittman Collaborative*

The Laboratory of Art and Ideas at Belmar
Lakewood, Colorado
2006

Brentwood Residence
Los Angeles, California
2007

Hotel Ray (unbuilt)
Venice, California
2007

Skyline Residence
Los Angeles, California
2007

Plaza Cafe at LACMA
Los Angeles, California
2008

Conga Room at L.A. Live
Los Angeles, California
2008

Las Lomas Residence
Los Angeles, California
2008

Pentimento at LACMA (unbuilt)
Los Angeles, California
2008

Selma Offices (unbuilt)
Los Angeles, California
2008

Holocaust Museum LA
Los Angeles, California
2010

Kona Residence
Kona, Hawaii
2010

20th Street Offices
Santa Monica, California
2010

Bar Toscana, Brentwood Village
Los Angeles, California
2011

Toronto Residence
Toronto, Ontario, Canada
2011

McKinnon Center for Global Affairs at Occidental College
Los Angeles, California
2013

Johnson Hall at Occidental College
Los Angeles, California
2013

Rising Glen Residence
Los Angeles, California
2013

Andaz Palm Springs*
Palm Springs, California
2014

Gores Group Headquarters
Beverly Hills, California
2014

The Agency Headquarters
Beverly Hills, California
2014

Pizzeria Prova
West Hollywood, California
2014

Woodside Residence (unbuilt)
Woodside, California
2014

The Pavilion at City of Hope
Duarte, California
2015

Tree Top Residence
Los Angeles, California
2015

Armenian American Museum Competition (unbuilt)
Glendale, California
2015

New Medical School Competition (unbuilt)
Pasadena, California
2015

Main + Hollister
Santa Monica, California
2016

Threads
Mexico City, Mexico
2016

Taller Estrella Jafif**
Mexico City, Mexico
2016

Tigertail Residence (unbuilt)
Los Angeles, California
2016

Arena Blanca Hotel (unbuilt)
Puerto Vallarta, Mexico
2017

Edges Residence
Los Angeles, California
2017

Nerano Restaurant
Beverly Hills, California
2017

Omaha Headquarters Competition (unbuilt)
Omaha, Nebraska
2017

Bridge Residence
Los Angeles, California
2018

Camelback Residence
Paradise Valley, Arizona
2018

***Design Architect only*

Profiles
Mexico City, Mexico
2018

Olive Residence
Los Angeles, California
2019

USC Shoah Foundation
Los Angeles, California
2019

West Olympic Science Hub (unbuilt)
Los Angeles, California
2019

Aurora (unbuilt)
Mexico City, Mexico
2020

BAR Center at the Beach
Los Angeles, California
2021

Bel Air Residence (unbuilt)
Los Angeles, California
2020

3205 Pico Boulevard
Santa Monica, California
2020

9350 Wilshire Boulevard
Beverly Hills, California
2020

2740 Main Street
Santa Monica, California
2021 (anticipated)

Apertures
Mexico City, Mexico
2021

Muskoka Cottage
Ontario, Canada
2021 (anticipated)

Sierra Mar Residence
Los Angeles, California
2021

Wallace Ridge Residence
Beverly Hills, California
2021

Holocaust Museum LA Expansion
Los Angeles, California
2022 (anticipated)

Lytton Residence
Ontario, Canada
2022 (anticipated)

1550 Euclid Street
Santa Monica, California
2022 (anticipated)

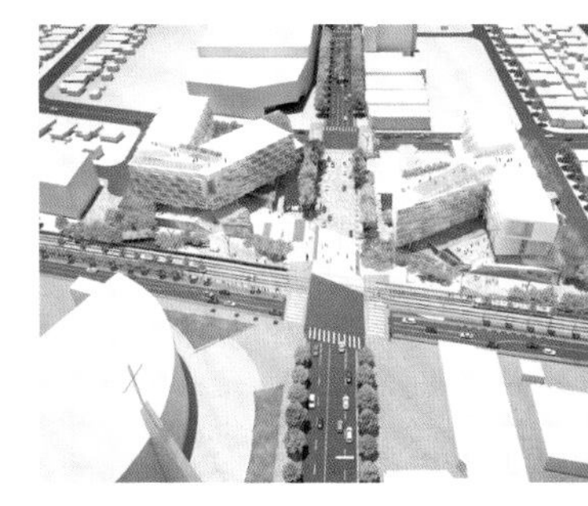

Crenshaw Crossing
Los Angeles, California
2023 (anticipated)

26th Street Offices
Santa Monica, California
2024 (anticipated)

STAFF
Past and Present

Christopher Arntzen
Andrew Atwood
Kelly Bair
Hagy Belzberg
Jane Belzberg
Micah Belzberg
Carina Bien-Wilner
Bill Bowen
Justin Brechtel
Susie Carnes
David Cheung
Carol Choi
Ashley Coon
Adrian Cortez
Jennifer Davis
Manish Desai
Brock DeSmit
Chuck Diep
Chuck Donlon
Chiara Ferrari
Jennifer Fontenot
Melanie Freeland
Barry Gartin
Glenn Ginter
Lindsay Green
J. Joshua Hanley
Josie Harrington
Isabel Hermann
Alice Hernandez Farkas
Suyun Jessica Hong
Mingyue Hu
Sungmi Hyun
Tianyu Kan
Andrew Kim
Minah Kim
Benjamin Kolder
Brad Lang
Danielle LeBouty
Elizabeth Lee
Philip Lee
Seren P. Lee
Kristofer Leese
Aaron Leppanen
Aaron Leshtz
Toni Lewis
Shen Li
Erin McCook
Amy Malheiros
Katelyn Miersma
Devon Montminy
Carolina Murcia
Camilla Neilson
Susan Nwankpa Gillespie
Joseph Ramiro
Daniel Rentsch
Alexis Roohani
Eduardo Ruvalcaba
Benjamin Sachs
Chris Sanford
Corie Saxman
Marc Schoeplein
Amanda Schwarz
Lindsey Sherman Contento
Erik Sollom
Eric Stimmel
Joy Stingone
Javier Suarez
Bryant Suh
Chris Tallon
Cory Taylor
Ryan Thomas
Filipa Valente
Anna Walley
Derrick Washington
George Wittman
Jennifer Wu
Melissa Yip
Taoran Zhao
Lauren Zuzack

Belzberg Architects' workspace opens to a large deck, taking advantage of the Santa Monica climate and offering opportunities for collaboration. Featured is one of a series of bespoke murals by artist Tommii Lim.

ACKNOWLEDGMENTS

The work represented in this monograph explores the culmination of a twenty-year collaboration between architects, designers, engineers, specialists, and contractors. This work would never have been possible without the alchemy of their talent, commitment, vision, and friendship. I especially thank our clients for their willingness to allow us to take chances, experiment, and ultimately, for their confidence in our investigations. I am humbled by my life partner, Jane Segal Belzberg, whose intellect illuminates every corner of the practice, and by Sara and Zack, for their extraordinary ability to keep me agile, and for their enduring love and patience despite the myriad conference calls, vacations cut short, and late nights at the office.

I am forever grateful to my partners, Dan Rentsch, Brock DeSmit, Cory Taylor, David Cheung, and Jen Wu, all of whom contain the rarest of ingredients needed to practice thoughtful and impassioned architecture. We are fortunate to be supported by our community of extraordinarily talented innovators: Chris Arntzen, Carol Choi, Jenny Fontenot, Barry Gartin, Alice Hernandez, Jessica Hong, Sungmi Hyun, Andrew Kim, Elizabeth Lee, Kris Leese, Aaron Leppanen, Susan Nwankpa, Amanda Schwarz, and Lindsey Sherman Contento. I am continually awed by their exceptional ability to manage ephemeral ideas and bring them to physical fruition. I humbly thank Susie Carnes for keeping me sane, along with Danielle LeBouty and Anna Walley; they are the grounding element without which our energetic and exuberant family could not thrive. Additional thanks go to Josh Hanley, Emma Hu, Tianyu Kan, Minah Kim, Ben Kolder, Shen Li, Devon Montminy, Corie Saxman, Melissa Yip, and Taoran Zhao, whose staggering talent is equaled by their design curiosity. It would be impossible to name every member of BA since its founding, but I am keenly aware that all our successes have been built upon the contributions of every single member of our studio since 1997. I also would like to extend my deepest gratitude to Alberto Djaddah, in whom I have found a dear friend and collaborator, and to all at Grupo Anima, whose trust in our studio and willingness to push us to unimaginable realms of exploration allowed us to create works beyond our wildest dreams.

I would further like to thank Sandra Gilbert Freidus and the incredible team at Rizzoli International Publications for partnering with us on our first office monograph.

I am profoundly indebted to the brilliant and seemingly inexhaustible Cindy Allen who encourages me with her keen insight and enthusiasm to never be complacent and to always challenge any perceived limits. And finally, I am grateful to Edie Cohen, who magnanimously gave me a second chance on a rainy day a long time ago, for her beautifully written words, generosity, and continued support.

—Hagy Belzberg

AUTHOR BIOGRAPHIES

CINDY ALLEN, Hon. IIDA, is widely lauded as one of the most influential advocates for the interior design profession. As editor-in-chief of *Interior Design* for almost two decades, Allen champions the industry, promoting both the giants of design and its rising stars. A self-proclaimed design junkie, she brings an unbridled passion for design that is manifested through eighteen print issues each year, a digital platform reaching a global audience of more than nine million, and a robust events platform. Allen has served as juror for the Cooper Hewitt National Design Awards and the Gensler Design Excellence Awards, as well as numerous other awards, is a board member of The Alpha Workshops, and is the chief design officer at SANDOW.

SARAH AMELAR is a journalist and author, with a particular focus on architecture, design, and cities. She holds a Master of Architecture degree from Yale University and has practiced with several firms, including Cesar Pelli and Associates and Michael Sorkin Studio. For a decade, she was a senior editor at *Architectural Record*, as well chief editor of *Record Houses* and *Record Interiors*, the magazine's annual awards issues. She has contributed to *The Phaidon Atlas of 21st Century World Architecture* and co-authored *Thomas Phifer and Partners* (Rizzoli International Publications, 2010) and *Where to Bike Los Angeles* (BA Press, 2012). Her articles have appeared in such publications as the *New York Times*, *Los Angeles Times*, *Architectural Record*, *Metropolis*, *Dwell*, *Architecture*, *Azure*, *Frame*, *Wallpaper*, *San Francisco Magazine*, and *Arquitectura Viva*. She is currently a contributing editor and frequent contributor to *Architectural Record*.

SAM LUBELL has written eight books about architecture, including *California Captured: Mid-Century Modern Architecture* (co-authored) and *Mid-Century Modern Architecture Travel Guide: West Coast USA* (both Phaidon Press, 2018). He is a contributing editor to *The Architect's Newspaper* and writes for the *New York Times*, *Wallpaper*, *Dwell*, *Wired*, the *Los Angeles Times*, *The Atlantic*, *Architectural Record*, *Architect Magazine*, *Contract*, *Architectural Review*, and other publications. Lubell has also curated architectural exhibitions, including *Never Built Los Angeles* (A+D Architecture and Design Museum, Los Angeles, 2013) and the subsequent *Never Built New York* (Queens Museum, New York, 2017).

HAGY BELZBERG, FAIA, received a Master of Architecture with Distinction from Harvard University (1991) and a Bachelor of Science from Arizona State University (1987). He founded Belzberg Architects in Santa Monica, California in 1997, shortly after completing an internship with Frank Gehry Associates. He has held an American Institute of Architects (AIA) directorship and graduate teaching positions at UCLA, USC, and SCI-Arc, where he continues to lecture and serve as a guest critic. In 2010, Belzberg was confirmed into the College of Fellows of the AIA for "Notable contributions to the advancement of the profession of architecture," recognized as an "Emerging Voice" by the Architectural League of New York, designated "Emerging Talent" from the AIA California, and was inducted into the *Interior Design* Hall of Fame in 2014. Belzberg Architects has received 115 prestigious national and international architecture and design awards including over thirty local, state, and national AIA awards. The work of Belzberg Architects was included in *A New Sculpturalism: Contemporary Architecture from Southern California*, at the Museum of Contemporary Art, Los Angeles and is featured in over 200 publications in more than twenty countries.

IMAGE CREDITS

+imgs: page 267 (1D)
Iwan Baan: pages 12 (ABOVE RIGHT), 62, 73, 75, 76, 77, 78, 79, 101, 103, 104, 106, 107, 108, 109, 265 (3A)
Belzberg Architects: pages 21, 22, 35, 67, 68, 74, 105, 116, 134 (BELOW), 179 (ABOVE), 246, 247, 249, 264 (1D), 265 (1C, 1E, 2C, 2D), 266 (1B, 2A, 2B, 3C), 267 (2C, 2D, 2E, 3C, 3D, 3E)
Berlyn Photography: pages 36, 37, 365 (1D)
Tom Bonner: page 264 (2E, 3B, 3C)
Benny Chan/Fotoworks: pages 6, 7, 12 (ABOVE LEFT), 13, 16, 17, 18, 23, 24, 26, 27, 28, 29, 30, 31, 33, 38, 39, 40, 41, 42, 43, 44, 45, 46, 47, 48, 53, 54, 55, 56, 57, 58, 59, 60, 61, 66, 69, 70, 71, 72, 82 (BELOW), 85, 86, 87, 89, 92, 93, 94, 95, 96, 97, 98, 99, 120, 121, 122, 123, 124, 126, 127, 128, 129, 130, 135, 139, 140, 141, 264 (2B, 2D, 3D), 265 (1B, 2A, 3B, 3C, 3F, 4E), 266 (3D)
Bruce Damonte: pages 12 (ABOVE CENTER), 15, 81, 82 (ABOVE), 110, 111, 112, 117, 118, 119, 125, 134 (ABOVE), 136, 137, 138, 142, 143, 145, 148, 149, 150, 151, 152, 153, 154, 155, 190, 191, 193, 195, 197, 198, 199, 200, 201, 202, 203, 204, 205, 206, 207, 208, 212, 213, 214, 215, 216, 217, 218, 219, 220, 221, 222, 223, 265 (4D), 266 (1A, 1C, 1D, 4C, 4D), 267 (1B, 1C)
Joel Eden Photography: page 265 (1A)
Farca+Grappin: page 266 (3B)
Art Gray: pages 8, 9, 224, 225, 226, 227, 229, 230, 233, 234, 235, 236, 237, 238, 239, 264 (2A), 265 (3D), 266 (2C, 4A), 267 (2A), 269
Grupo Anima: page 267 (1E)
Roland Halbe: pages 158, 161, 163, 165, 166, 167, 168, 169, 170, 171, 266 (2D)
Ben Rahn/A-Frame: page 265 (3A)
LGM Studio: dustjacket, pages 83, 156,157, 164, 172, 173, 175, 179 (BELOW), 180, 181, 182, 183, 184, 185, 186, 187, 188, 189, 240, 241, 242, 250, 251, 252, 253, 254, 255, 256, 257, 258, 259, 260, 261, 262, 263, 266 (3A), 267 (1A, 3A)
Polynates: pages 266 (4B), 267 (2B, 3B, 4A, 4B, 4C)
PUBLIC: page 267 (4D)
Spine3D: page 265 (4C)
Tim Street-Porter: pages 11, 264 (1A, 1B, 1C, 1E)
Taiyo Watanabe: page 265 (2B, 4A, 4B)
Unknown: page 264 (2C, 3A)

**For the Project Chronology credits, image row and column are designated by number top to bottom and letter left to right, respectively.*

First published in the United States of America in 2021 by Rizzoli International Publications, Inc.
300 Park Avenue South
New York, NY 10010
www.rizzoliusa.com

Publisher: Charles Miers
Project Editor: Sandra Gilbert Freidus
Editorial Assistance: Sara Pozefsky and Stephanie Salomon
Design: Carol Choi, Shen Li, David Cheung, and Jessica Hong, Emma Hu, Sungmi Hyun, Tianyu Kan, Minah Kim, Benjamin Kolder, Corie Saxman, Melissa Yip, Taoran Zhao
Production Manager: Maria Pia Gramaglia
Managing Editor: Lynn Scrabis
Cover Design: Shen Li, David Cheung, Emma Hu

Printed in Italy

2021 2022 2023 2024 / 10 9 8 7 6 5 4 3 2 1
ISBN: 978-0-8478-7004-2
Library of Congress Control Number: 2021937244

Visit us online:
Facebook.com/RizzoliNewYork
instagram.com/rizzolibooks
twitter.com/Rizzoli_Books
pinterest.com/rizzolibooks
youtube.com/user/RizzoliNY
issuu.com/Rizzoli